UPON FURTHER REVIEW

Controversy in Sports Officiating

Blair Kerkhoff

ADDAX
PUBLISHING
GROUP

Number 10, former Minnesota Vikings quarterback Fran Tarkenton, watches a measurement intently. The gentleman in the coat to his immediate right was known for intensity, too – legendary Packers coach Vince Lombardi. *(Photo by Vernon Biever.)*

Nelson Elliott
Managing Editor

Judy Widener
Editor

Randy Breeden
Art Direction/Design

Dustjacket design by Laura Bolter

Published by Addax Publishing Group, Inc.
Copyright © 2000 Blair Kerkhoff

ISBN: 1-886110-84-0

Printed in the U.S.A

1 3 5 7 9 10 8 6 4 2

Library of Congress Cataloging-in-Publication Data

Kerkhoff, Blair, 1959-
  Upon further review : controversy in sports officiating / Blair Kerkhoff.
    p. cm.
  ISBN 1-886110-84-0 (hc)
  1. Sports officiating—United States. I. Title.
GV735.K47 1999
                                          99-055083

DEDICATION

To the men in blue, stripes, zebras and all other species of officials.

There are no games without you.

TABLE OF CONTENTS

ACKNOWLEDGMENTS

The best part of writing a book is finishing. The second best is having the opportunity to thank the people who made the book possible.

I wasn't sure how much cooperation I'd get from officials who usually talk to reporters only in post-game situations and only to interpret a ruling. Once in a while you'll read a profile of an official in a game program or magazine and many have related their experiences in autobiographies. But to open up about the issues, some controversial, in today's game, it would be of little benefit for men and women working the games. Most contacted politely declined.

We had more luck with former officials, whose observations are valuable. Steve Palermo, a former American League umpire, has worked with the commissioner's office since a gunshot wound ended his career in 1991. Few outside the game were closer or had more knowledge of the umpires' battles, not only in 1999, but since the Roberto Alomar spitting incident. Palermo has much to offer baseball and should be a permanent part of Commissioner Bud Selig's staff.

I met former NFL referee Jim Tunney at the 1999 College Football Hall of Fame induction ceremony in South Bend, Ind. He was the keynote speaker for a class that included Bo Jackson, Jim McMahon and Tom Osborne. He did a terrific job, which isn't surprising. He's turned public speaking into a business among his many enterprises. Look for his latest book, *Chicken Soup for the Sports Fan Soul.*

Former NFL referee Jerry Markbreit, who has written two books, former boxing referee Mills Lane, famous for calling the Tyson-

Holyfield ear-biting bout, and Final Four referee Scott Thornley provided valuable insights about their profession and careers.

Barry Mano is the publisher and executive editor of *Referee* magazine, a complete source of information about the officiating profession. If you're an official and aren't getting *Referee* you're cheating yourself. Officials who don't tell their stories to news organizations tell them to *Referee*. There's more journalistic integrity in the magazine than you'd expect of a specialty publication. Bill Dwyre, sports editor of *The Los Angeles Times* and a giant in the sports journalism business, is a regular columnist.

Mano is working hard to create awareness for a growing problem in officiating, abuse. It's out of hand and getting worse, especially at the recreation and youth levels. In October, 1999, news anchors got a laugh out of a story in Ohio where parents took a vow of silence during youth soccer games. Some taped their mouths, others sucked candy, but nobody said anything to the officials or players. The reaction from them was priceless. Kids were smiling and the officials called action free from yelling parents. Even parents agreed the level of play and officiating was better. And the whole thing was more fun than usual.

John Erickson, the former Big Eight supervisor of officials, Roger Morningstar, former college basketball standout who runs a recreation center, and Dr. Roy Askins, a psychology professor at Western Nevada State, provided expertise in their fields and are good friends of the officiating profession.

Many thanks to *The Kansas City Star* executive sports editor Mike Fannin, who lent his support for the project from its origin.

ACKNOWLEDGMENTS

The idea for this book belongs to Nelson Elliott of Addax Publishing. We sat in the office of Addax president Bob Snodgrass and started listing the issues in officiating today and before long convinced ourselves it was a story worth telling. We had to work fast and nothing came easily. Thanks to Nelson, Bob and everybody at Addax for their patience. Also, thanks to Judy Widener, who handled the dirty work, the editing.

I am able to undertake projects because of the love and understanding of my family. Karen and the kids, Nate, Ben and Anna make everything worthwhile.

INTRODUCTION

Deep down we're all officials.

Watch any sporting event, even one in which you have no emotional investment in the outcome, and at some point you'll be overcome by the urge to officiate. "He called that a strike? That's obviously pass interference. How many steps did he take? We won in spite of the officials. Officials cost us the game."

More sophisticated observers take it to another level. During a recent college basketball game, I sat next to a sportswriter who before the first TV timeout announced the officials had lost control of the game and we were about to witness 40 minutes of brutal, playground type action. The writer apparently didn't consider that the lead official was Don Rutledge, one of the game's most respected referees. In a tight, tense struggle, Rutledge twice teed up the opposing coach and sent him to the locker room. Losing control? It was never an issue.

The same cannot be said for the officiating profession lately. Referees, umpires and officials made more news in the final years of the 20th century than at any other time in history. These are extraordinary times for a profession that ultimately succeeds when it blends into the action and the identity of the official doesn't matter.

But it mattered in a big way in baseball stadiums from the 1999 All-Star break until September 2. In those seven weeks, many crews consisted of a mixed bag of umpires loyal to the union, umpires who despised the union leader and replacement umpires

15

who were about to step in full-time for veterans who had tendered their resignations.

It mattered in the NFL. When Phil Luckett's crew was assigned to a game in 1999, fans knew this was the guy who blew the coin toss and the Vinny Testaverde touchdown the previous year. The fact that Luckett didn't blow either call wasn't important to fans. They were getting "bad" Luckett's crew.

It mattered in the NBA. Were these the officials Dennis Rodman head-butted or Nick Van Exel shoved over the scorer's table? It mattered in college basketball. Is this the official who's had it in for Bobby Knight?

All of a sudden, we all wanted to know who was calling the game and how it might factor in the action and outcome. It didn't used to be that way, at least not on a fan's level. That was before officials started making the front pages.

Upon Further Review offers a sportswriter's unbiased interpretation of some of the events involving officials that pushed the profession out of the background and uncomfortably into the spotlight. It's a snapshot of some of the most important issues in officiating in the late 1990s written by somebody who has always respected the profession and has dabbled in it on the recreational level.

I've covered sports for two decades and have usually practiced caution when dealing in print with calls that upset fans. That doesn't mean not identifying the referee who made the critical touch-foul call 80 feet from the basket with six seconds left in a one-point game. But I have worked with coaches who have had problems with particular officials and wanted to undermine their credibility with some indirect comments.

Sorry. I suppose the next time I see a coach return the bounty of an official's mistake then I'll begin to consider particular gripes. I thought one of the most offensive images for officials in the past few years occurred when one of my favorite coaches, Bill Cowher of the Pittsburgh Steelers, stuffed a photograph into the referee's pocket before running off at halftime. The photo caught an official's error. I wanted to see the official stuff a photograph of some failed fourth-down gamble into Cowher's pocket.

Believe it or not, at times throughout history, honesty was the most important issue in a ball game. A century ago, umpires could ask fans closer to the action if a ball was fair or foul. In one of the most celebrated acts of sportsmanship, Cornell coach Carl Snavely surrendered a victory to Dartmouth when he learned his team had scored the winning touchdown on a fifth down. Fifty years later, Colorado wouldn't have dreamed of forfeiting its victory over Missouri under the same circumstances.

Have we changed that much? In some ways we haven't changed at all. Not long after umpires were asking fans to weigh in on the rules, baseball became a savage game and umpires were caught in the middle. They were common targets of physical and verbal abuse. Today, at the youth and recreational level, incidents of violence against officials is so prevalent states have enacted laws to specifically protect them.

As my attendance at youth league games multiplies yearly with my growing children, I've never witnessed an umpire physically abused. But I have noticed the effect on kids when dads and moms unleash verbal assaults on umpires. Suddenly, kids who never questioned whether they were safe or out or if a pitch was a ball or strike, come back to the dugout complaining about the umpiring. For some kids I know, an enduring image of the past baseball season wasn't a base hit or nice catch but a coach screaming in the face of a trembling teenage umpire with a bleacher of parents supporting his cause. The players were 8 and 9.

One of the ideas of this project was to explore some of the issues that fascinate fans. Are there make-up calls? Are games called differently in the final seconds of a close game than in earliest moments? How much influence can a loud home crowd have? Do stars get favored treatment? But officials I talked to formally and informally all said the same thing. Officials don't have time to consider make-up calls; the definition of a foul or a penalty doesn't change during the course of a game; fans don't influence calls but officials hear them; and stars are stars because they know how to avoid trouble situations.

About the latter, former NBA head of officials Darell Garretson probably said it best. "Officials don't meet before the season and say 'We're going to elevate him to superstar status.' If it appears the refs are giving them some type of breaks I'd like for someone to point out what it is. I wish we were that intelligent where we could say 'Oh, that's so and so. He's not supposed to have those calls against him, so I won't call it.' Superstars make themselves look good. They don't need any help from us."

Perhaps those are textbook answers that don't square with your idea of reality. But we couldn't find enough contradiction to build a case. Voices from some of the best officials in sports history comment on today's issues.

There are some descriptions of controversial calls, a short history of the profession and a roll call of some of the most honored officials. Moments like the call that turned the 1908 pennant race between the New York Giants and Chicago Cubs and the long count in the 1926 heavyweight title fight between Gene Tunney and Jack Dempsey are woven into the fabric of sports lore and are replayed here.

Halls of Fame generally have been slow to recognize officials. It took baseball 14 years to enshrine umpires and the first five in also had worked in the league office. Basketball did a much better job recognizing its officials. Six referees were inducted among the Hall's first three classes. But only one official who has worked in the NBA in the last 40 years, Earl Strom, is in the Hall.

At least basketball, baseball and ice hockey recognize officials. Football shamefully does not. Officials are eligible and have been nominated. But the 36-member voting board has not seen fit to place an official along side the owners, coaches and players. It's a slap to guys like Red Cashion, Jim Tunney, Norm Schachter and Jerry Markbreit and others widely considered the best in the game's history, and a slap at the profession, to go unrecognized in Canton, Ohio.

Officials won't find a lack of respect here. I hope they enjoy the book. I hope you enjoy the book, too.

Blair Kerkhoff

"The human being is not really made to respect discipline automatically, especially when the passions are raised and the prospect of winning often becomes more important than how we play the game. In our modern society, the referee is both the one capable of controlling violence but also the one who may inadvertently incite it by a single decision, justified or not."

- Michel Vautrot, Hall of Fame soccer official

Chapter 1

BASEBALL

THE SPIT HITS THE FAN
AND THE UMPIRES STRIKE BACK

Quitting time?

The Oakland A's visited Kansas City for a three-game series in late July, but the games were almost an afterthought. It was the weekend of Royals favorite son George Brett's induction to the Hall of Fame. Most of the team's front office personnel and even a coach were off to Cooperstown.

But the umpires were making news of their own. Two weeks earlier, the day after the All-Star Game, 57 of 68 umpires resigned in an attempt to force an early start to negotiations before their collective bargaining agreement expired December 31. Little did the umpires know, this tactic would be a high-stakes gamble that 22 umpires ultimately would lose.

American League umpire Mike Reilly weighed his loyalty to the union against supporting his family and love of his job. He had withdrawn his resignation only hours before working the opener of the A's-Royals series. It hurt to talk about it. But the idea of ending a 23-year major league career and losing a six-figure salary pained him even more.

"I have a family — four young children and a wife," Reilly said. "I looked at the possibility of not having a job. I had to do this for my wife and kids."

In an apparent trend among American League umpires, Reilly and others withdrew their resignations because they didn't like the hard-line negotiating style of union leader Richie Phillips. The first to withdraw resignations were AL umps Rocky Roe, Larry Barnett, Dave Phillips, Jim Joyce and Dale Scott, who also resigned from the union board.

The next wave of withdrawals included Chuck Merriwether and Gary Cederstrom of the AL and Wally Bell and Jeff Nelson of the National League. Then came Rick Reed, Tim Tschida and Larry Young, who issued this joint statement: "In light of the difficulties of the past week, we have decided to honor the present terms of our contract."

At the time, Reilly made it 12 AL umps and 14 overall to withdraw resignations. Added to the 12 who didn't resign in the first place, baseball was headed to the September 2 deadline with this scoreboard: 42 umpires resigned, 14 resigned but withdrew, and 12 didn't resign. Finally, there was AL ump Greg Kosc, who resigned, withdrew and resigned again.

When it became obvious baseball wasn't going to deal with the umpires, that resignations were what the game wanted, the umps had lost. Phillips had miscalculated baseball's response. He didn't anticipate baseball would view the action as an opportunity to thin the ranks, even if some of the game's best and most respected umps, like the American League's Richie Garcia, were lost in the process. The commissioner's office hired 25 new umpires, primarily from Class AAA, to fill the roster.

As the deadline approached, the saga took many twists and turns, none more bizarre than the August day the umpires sued baseball for the right to withdraw their resignations. The 14-page complaint accused the American League and commissioner's office of threatening to withhold termination pay. The suit also alleged baseball offered umpires a cash incentive to join a "Dump Phillips" movement.

But baseball was able to choose from among the resignations which ones it wanted to accept. In the end, 13 NL umpires and nine in the American League lost their jobs. Among them were some of the game's longest-tenured veterans. NL ump Frank Pulli had been on the staff since 1972, and was planning to retire after the 2000 season. "Is this what I deserve after 28 years?" Pulli asked.

The umpires who quit filed unfair labor practice charges against baseball. Phillips asked the National Labor Relations Board to seek an injunction in federal court to prevent baseball from forcing out the umps. In a similar process in 1994, players filed an injunction against the owners that caused the union to end its strike of over seven months duration.

Each arbiter wrestled with his conscience.

"It was one of the toughest decisions I've made in my life," said Reilly. He then headed down the corridor in Kauffman Stadium and prepared to work a game with Mark Johnson, who hadn't resigned, and a pair of umpires hired this year.

This umpiring crew, like many others, represented the ideological rift of the most divisive season in the history of officiating. Certainly, it was the most calamitous year in the proud century of umpiring. By the end of the 1999 season, the umpires union, which had known only labor victories in the previous two decades, had all but crumbled.

On the evening of September 2, several of the game's best worked their final innings. In St. Louis, Pulli pretended to make one final ejection. When the game ended, Cardinals first baseman Mark McGwire gave Pulli the game ball.

"If (Pulli's) one of the worst 22 umpires in this league, I'm a kamikaze pilot," Marlins manager Rene Lachemann told reporters after the game. "It's a big mistake they fired him."

Kosc, a 23-year veteran, had tears in his eyes as he accepted the lineup cards before an Orioles-Devil Rays game. As he left the field, he shook hands with Baltimore manager Ray Miller, Tampa Bay manager Larry Rothchild and Orioles outfielder Brady Anderson. "I told him, thanks for all the years of being so professional," Miller said.

Three umpires — crew chief Terry Tata, Bill Hohn and Tom Hallion — worked their final game at a Dodgers-Brewers meeting in Los Angeles. After the eighth inning, the Dodger Stadium organist paid tribute to the umpires with a rendition of "I'll Be Seeing You."

"It not only has broken my heart, but it has devastated me as an individual," Hallion said after the game. "I just did my last game. This is what I want to do, this is what I love to do. I love baseball. But right now, I hate baseball."

Emotions also got the better of Hohn.

"Don't these baseball people have any hearts?" he asked. "We have families. They're ruining families, and that's what hurts. It was a mistake, but my God, we're good people. We're the integrity of the game."

Threatening letters

Reilly assured the public that dissension among the umpiring ranks wouldn't spill onto the field, and to the umps' credit, that appeared to be true. There were no outward signs of strain between the strong union umps and those who withdrew their resignations.

Off the field, it was a different story. Tata, a 27-year veteran, referred to those who withdrew as "scabs," saying, "If there's a small fire on the ship, you put it out. You don't jump overboard into the water with the sharks."

Sadly, the bitter feelings spilled over into relationships among families. Marcia Montague, wife of NL ump Ed Montague, called AL umpire John Hirschbeck "Judas" in a letter to his wife, Denise Hirschbeck. Hirschbeck and AL umpire Joe Brinkman were blamed by Phillips for organizing the opposition group.

Hirschbeck and Brinkman had sought advice about the conflict from sports agent Ron Shapiro, a Baltimore attorney and Cal Ripken's agent. Shapiro had been chosen by a group of AL umpires to replace Phillips in February. But the vote went 49-14 for the status quo, and Phillips received a new five-year contract reportedly worth $300,000.

Montague's letter read: "You must be very proud of your husband's efforts to undermine 20 years of work from an association that has reaped him so many benefits. It's a shame, because it would have been a good fight against what's wrong in baseball. Maybe we all could have made a difference in the fight to restore real leadership to the game. I would have liked to see us take on the MLB, the commissioner and the media for promoting the myths that umpires are arrogant when they are actually proud; that they are not accountable when they always have been — to the leagues and to themselves.

"But we didn't see the Judas in our midst, who sold us out for 20 pieces of gold. I guess you'll have to live with that. And John will, too, every time he walks onto the field. And your kids will, when you teach them about ethics and morals. And so will all the other umpires and their wives and children who followed John because they believed in ... what?

"John is an embarrassment to all real umpires and baseball because he forgot the quintessential — baseball is a team sport and he thinks he is bigger than the team. He shamed us all. I can say my husband was good for the game. Can you?"

Copies of this scathing letter were sent to every umpire's wife, prompting baseball to warn umpires not to harass each other. AL

President Gene Budig and NL President Len Coleman issued memos to umpires warning them of disciplinary measures for noncompliance.

After the resignations were accepted, an unsigned letter was delivered to the 25 umpires who opposed Richie Phillips. The letter was postmarked August 31 from Santa Ana, Calif., and read:

"How could you jump out of the foxhole in the midst of battle and desert your friends for your own selfishness? How could you pledge your allegiance to the 'intelligence' of Joe Brinkman, Mark Hirschbeck and John Hirschbeck? How could you forget that all you have is due to collective bargaining, done by Richie Phillips for you?

"If you didn't agree with the resignation idea, why didn't you have the courage to oppose it at the July 14 meeting?

"Remember — you abandoned the ship! You sunk the ship! Now you have to look at yourself in the mirror every day, forever and see the reflection of a cowardly, selfish scab!

"You can change. You can return your allegiance where it belongs."

These letters were among the stories that kept umpires in the headlines throughout the season of discontent.

A four-year fuse

So how did the umpires find themselves in this mess? There had been strikes, walkouts, protests and picket lines since the union was formed in the 1960s. Umpires missed the first six weeks of play in 1979, sat out most openers in 1991, and were locked out the first eight days of 1995. Each time, issues were settled, hands were shaken, and hard feelings were left at the bargaining table.

Then came a shameful episode in baseball history, a moment that defined the game's ugliness. The event became a wound baseball allowed to fester. If it hadn't happened, the umpires might not have found themselves battling baseball.

The miserable relations between umpires and baseball began seconds after John Hirschbeck called a strike on a pitch that appeared to be outside. During the second game of the 1996 American League first-round playoff series, Roberto Alomar of the Baltimore Orioles spat in the face of John Hirschbeck. The action ranks with the most hideous and cowardly by an athlete toward an official. But the American League's punishment, which amounted to a slap on the wrist, was the main problem. Umpires felt baseball's respect and support for their authority had eroded.

Alomar protested the call, Hirschbeck allegedly called him a name, and Alomar unloaded the contents of his mouth. After the game, Alomar explained his spitting by saying Hirschbeck once had been a nice guy, but that he wasn't the same arbiter since his 8-year-old son had died of a rare brain disease. Upon hearing this, Hirschbeck attempted to confront Alomar in the Orioles' locker room, but was restrained.

For one of the few times in sports history, public sympathy landed squarely on the side of the official. America was outraged at Alomar. By coincidence, the episode occurred in the midst of a presidential campaign. During a nationally-televised vice-presidential debate, moderator Jim Lehrer asked candidates Al Gore and Jack Kemp about the situation. He wondered, "Has something gone terribly wrong with the American soul, that we've become too mean, too selfish?"

Kemp sidestepped the issue, but Gore's response may have been his high point of the evening: "I think (Alomar) should have been severely disciplined, suspended, perhaps, immediately. I don't understand why that action was not taken."

AL President Gene Budig suspended Alomar for five games with pay at the beginning of the 1997 season. However, umpires wanted a longer suspension, and for Alomar to serve the penalty during the playoffs. They threatened to walk off the job unless the suspension was effective immediately. A crisis was averted when a federal judge barred the umps from striking.

However, the umps did what they could. The start of a Yankees-Rangers playoff game was delayed 10 minutes, and the Orioles-Indians game was held up 17 minutes in protest. They retaliated against Alomar immediately; he discovered his strike zone had suddenly swelled. Ironically, Baltimore won the first-round series over Cleveland on an Alomar homer in extra innings of the final game.

But in the first game of the AL Championship Series against the

Yankees, Alomar was the final out in the half-innings 1, 3, 5, 9 and 11. He got no calls. The squeeze-out by umps might have received more attention, but during that game, Richie Garcia missed a home-run interference call. Because of Garcia's lapse, a 12-year-old spectator turned a possible out into an eighth-inning game-tying homer by snatching the ball before it reached a Baltimore glove.

Ultimately, the umpires received no satisfaction in the Alomar incident. Budig's punishment clearly did not fit the crime, considering that in 1945, striking an umpire meant a lifetime ban from the game for the offending player or coach. In the late 1980s, the penalty was a one-month suspension for shoving an arbiter. The appeal that allowed Alomar to continue playing stung like a slap in the umpires' faces, a feeling that never went away.

"To a certain degree, the circumstances created this chasm," said former American League umpire Steve Palermo. "It was like catching a guy robbing a store a few days before Christmas and the judge saying, 'I'm going to let you go until January 4.' The playoffs are baseball's holiday season and Alomar wrongfully knocked Cleveland out of the playoffs.

"At some point in time, you have to be responsible for your actions. You have to be held accountable. Here's (Orioles owner) Peter Angelos. Do you think he really cared about the sanctity of the game when this happened? The American public was outraged. How could you tell your son to be like Robby Alomar after that?

"Baseball doesn't support (Hirschbeck). When I umpired, the

only thing I cared about was protecting the game. I kept in mind how good it's been to me my whole life. Then this happened, and I wonder who else is interested in protecting the game."

Beyond fortifying the notion that commissioner-less baseball (which occurred before Bud Selig was named to the post) existed with no true moral force, merely consisting of interest groups battling for power and position — the Alomar incident proved more harmful than anyone could have imagined. Oh, the careers of Alomar and Hirschbeck churned on. They even met early in the 1997 season, shook hands and tried to patch things up. But to umpires, severe damage had been done and repairs were not made during a February, 1997, summit among umpires, players, owners and then-acting commissioner Selig.

Umpires came into the meeting with two major demands. They wanted players to serve suspensions immediately when issued, rather than after appeals had been exhausted. They also wanted teams to withhold pay from suspended players. In essence, they were asking for their authority to be upheld. In these instances, owners said no. The meeting accomplished nothing.

Small skirmishes during the next two seasons fed the umpires' resentment. After the 1997 season, umpires were ordered by an arbitrator to use stopwatches between innings to ensure no pitches would be thrown before television coverage resumed following commercial breaks. Umpires argued that timing breaks wasn't covered by their collective bargaining agreement.

The strike zone, which can be as flexible as an umpire's personality, contorted into odd shapes during the 1997 post-season. For example, during one NL Championship Series game,

Marlins pitcher Livan Hernandez struck out 15 Atlanta Braves, many on pitches that sailed over the opposite batter's box. Coincidentally, the home plate arbiter, Eric Gregg, was one of the 22 umpires who didn't get his job back.

Interpretation of the strike zone became one of the umpire's hot-button topics before the 1999 season. Various issues soured the umpires' collective attitude and turned spring training into a major league distraction, paving the way for the July decision to walk off the job in September. Here is a brief review of the issues:

• Sandy Alderson, the new executive vice-president of baseball operations in the commissioner's office, released a memorandum February 19 directing umpires to raise the strike zone to two inches above the top of the uniform pants. However, the official rules define the strike zone as midpoint between the top of the shoulders and the top of the uniform pants. Richie Phillips went ballistic.

"In a misguided edict to raise the strike zone, the commissioner's office, in fact, substantially lowered the zone, and has done so in direct violation of the Major League Agreement, which requires a two-thirds vote of the rules committee to effect any rules change," Phillips said in a statement.

Also, Phillips complained that the umpire's labor agreement requires they be consulted regarding such changes. "Should the umpires comply with the new strike zone rule, they will be in violation of the Major League Agreement and their contractual obligations to enforce the official playing rules."

The umpires were upset about the fact that most of them were informed about the strike zone order through the media; more troublesome was that baseball had instructed teams to chart pitches, thereby monitoring the umpires.

"It's juvenile, it's nonsensical and it's a case of Big Brother watching over us," Phillips told *The New York Post*.

The umps called higher strikes during spring training, and some carried the practice into the regular season. Players noticed, but the problem seemed worse than when each of the 68 AL and NL umpires essentially had his own interpretation of the rule-book strike zone. The strike zone, as defined in the rule book, consists of the area over home plate and the midpoint between the top of the shoulders and the top of the uniform pants. Basically, it's armpits to knees.

• Consolidation of the AL and NL umpires under one administrative umbrella, which eliminated separate staffs, was seen by the umps as baseball's attempt to break the union. Under the revised system, the commissioner's office would be responsible for the firing, hiring, discipline, training and evaluation of umpires.

Why did baseball want this change? Officials correctly observed baseball is the only major professional sport with multiple training sources. The NFL, NBA and NHL each have one training program. The commissioner's office counted seven for baseball: separate programs for each league, the union, the minor leagues, and three umpiring schools developed and operated by major league umpires. All of these programs are interpreting the same rule book.

Another issue that concerned baseball was the umpire's expanding waistlines. Before the Reds-Expos opening game in 1996, 51-year-old John McSherry died of a massive heart attack, bringing the subject to light. McSherry was listed at 328 pounds. An Associated Press study found the average weight of NL umps was 214 pounds; average AL umps were 204. Eight checked in over 238.

"Do we have guys who are overweight? Yes," Phillips said in an interview with *USA Today Baseball Weekly.* "The leagues should do something about that. They should not penalize a guy. The leagues should have a staff who see to the physical well-being of the umpires. They should have people the umpires report to in each city. They should have training facilities.

"The clubs say to use the same facilities the players use. (Umpires) don't want to do that. They don't want to sit on a stationary bike next to a pitcher they called balls and strikes on last night."

• The same day they filed the strike zone grievance, the umpires fired off another to prevent the American League from sending a crew to work an exhibition series between the Baltimore Orioles and the Cuban national team. Umpires felt they should be paid for the trip, but they were told they would not receive additional compensation for making the trip because the Orioles and other baseball personnel weren't paid extra.

• Then came the kicker. March 30, newspapers published a best-to-worst ranking of umpires in both leagues. Every major league player received a copy of the survey, and managers and coaches were invited to participate. The umps were rated in several categories: physical condition, physical and mental toughness, accuracy of calls on the bases, accuracy of calls at the plate, consistency, temperament, respect for players and overall capacity.

The umpires didn't take the ratings seriously. They never have, unless the survey was conducted by fellow officials. Al Barlick dismissed a 1961 *Sporting News* ranking for that reason.

The release came on the heels of the strike zone and Cuba trip grievances along with a rumor that baseball wanted to fire umpires, which the commissioner's office denied. This survey struck a nerve.

The survey identified Tim McClelland, Jim Joyce and Richie Garcia as the American League's top three; Jerry Crawford, Ed Rapuano and Ed Montague were rated best in the National League. Ken Kaiser and Charlie Williams were at the bottom of the list in their respective leagues. The rankings irritated Phillips.

"If you take the top 68 neurosurgeons in the world and monitor their surgical skills and patient relations," Phillips said in the *USA Today* report, "even if you could find a good way of rating them, some are still going to rate 64 or 65 or 66, 67, 68. That doesn't mean they're bad neurosurgeons. They are still good, and they are head and shoulders above the majority of people."

Despite his status at the top of the list, Crawford, president of the Major League Umpires Association, was livid. Asked by *Referee* magazine why he thought the poll was conducted, Crawford was succinct. "They wanted to embarrass people ... I don't know who they were trying to get back at. I feel that it wasn't the smartest thing to do."

Players union chief Donald Fehr defended the poll, claiming players are in the best position to evaluate umps. Steve Palermo strongly disagreed.

"The only one who can rate an umpire is another umpire," Palermo asserted. "And most I know are honest enough to tell each other where they need to improve. They took the survey and had no intention of sharing the evaluation. I think they were getting (evidence) on umpires to fire them."

Also, Palermo wondered if one particular call influenced the voting, citing Don Denkinger's infamous 1985 World Series call that kept alive a Kansas City Royals' ninth-inning rally.

"You take a guy like Don Denkinger (23rd among AL umps). A top guy, in my opinion. He worked behind the plate for the 1978 playoff game between the Yankees and Red Sox. That's a tribute in our business. He has one bad call, the whole world sees it, and people think he's a bad umpire. You know, George Brett struck out in the ninth inning a few times in his career. Am I going to say Brett stinks? In that game in '78, you know who made the last out for Boston? Carl Yastrzemski pops out to Graig Nettles. Now, is Yaz a bad player? Of course not.

"I think that's how the survey worked. I like what Billy Martin once said when someone asked him about ranking umpires. He said we were all tied for last place."

However, few outside the umpiring profession would agree.

"There are bad umpires, no question about that," said Dr. Roy Askins, a former umpire, currently a psychology professor at Western Nevada College. "Anyone who has ever worked a game knows there are days when you don't have a feel for it. There are days when the best umpires are lousy, they can't find a corner. And there are days when average umpires are worse than that."

There was no peace between the umpires and baseball in the first half of 1999, and no peace among the men in blue for much of the second half. Umps were convinced baseball's strike zone edict, consolidation plan, Cuba trip and the survey were piled high in an attempt to crush the union. As the season opened, a strike or lockout was predicted when the umpires' labor agreement expired on the final day of the century.

No one was shocked when the season unfolded and umpires seemed more confrontational. One incident in particular may provide the clearest snapshot of the 1999 season. Tom Hallion was suspended for three games after bumping Colorado Rockies catcher Jeff Reed and coach Milt May in June. Hallion's resignation stuck and he was certain the incident gave baseball the ammunition it needed to boot him out.

Umpires were quick to point out Hallion received no pay during his suspension, while Alomar didn't lose a dime.

All-Star meeting

The mounting frustrations of umpires finally boiled over the day after the All-Star game in Boston, and the timing couldn't have been worse. With baseball still feeling flush from a highly successful extravaganza, the umpires dropped the bombshell.

During a meeting in Philadelphia, 57 umpires announced their resignation. September 2 was picked as the effective date because pennant races would be heating up, and umpires believed it was a time baseball could least afford replacements.

The resignation papers were ready for the umpires to sign upon their arrival. According to the *Boston Globe*, many umps were under the impression they would be taking a one-day wildcat strike, even though striking wasn't allowed under the terms of their contract. The mass resignation wasn't discussed in a conference call before the meeting, Phillips said, because he didn't want the news to leak out.

According to AL umpire Dave Phillips (no relation to Richie), no opposition to the resignations was raised at the Philadelphia meeting because the strategy was presented as no big deal. The resignations were simply to be used as a negotiating tool, and some umpires left the meeting believing the letters would not be mailed.

Dave Phillips recalled, "I said, 'This may be the best idea you've had since 1979,' " when Richie Phillips staged a strike that yielded umpires tremendous upgrades in working conditions. "He had intimated that the letters were never going to be sent."

Most umpires continued to trust Phillips, the son of a Philadelphia policeman. Phillips himself once served as chief of homicide for the city. He had played football for Villanova in the 1960s, and later coached its freshman football team. Besides his union job, Phillips is chairman, president and chief financial officer of the 1,500-employee Pilot Air Freight, based in Lima, Pa. The company was on the brink of declaring bankruptcy when he took over in 1994. Hundreds of jobs were saved when he turned the company around.

But according to one arbiter, Phillips lost a group of umpires the day they signed their resignations. When the umpires flew home or to their next assignments, they were confronted by reporters seeking comments on the mass resignation. Dave Phillips called it "mass suicide, like Jim Jones in Guyana."

There was no united front before the meeting started. Nine umpires didn't make it to Philadelphia. "What did they think when nine umpires didn't show?" Dave Phillips said. "Did they figure all these guys had flight connection problems? They were rebelling."

The announcement stunned baseball, but the umpires were stung when public perception lined up squarely against them. "Overpaid underachievers," one columnist called the umpires. "It's a union where they don't work for five months ... where no one has been fired for 20 years because of incompetence."

Final blow

As the 1999 regular season came to a close, the anti-Richie Phillips forces once again launched a campaign to dump the union leader. Signatures were collected from umpires to decertify the union and start a new one.

"We feel very confident there's a silent group that will look favorably on our approach to a new, open, democratic form of government that will unify this group," Dave Phillips said.

The group called itself the Major League Umpires Independent Organizing Committee. Several umpires in the group had issued a statement earlier in the summer condemning Richie Phillips.

"We want a union that does not encourage its members to follow flawed and dangerous strategies," the organization was quoted in a statement.

LABOR PAINS

The umpires' labor problems in 1999 were only the latest in a series of issues. The men in blue first blew their stack in 1925, threatening to strike over poor wages and working conditions. It never happened. In 1945, American League umpire Ernie Stewart was fired for union activity. But the last three decades have provided plenty of off-field action for umpires.

1964

The National League Umpires Association was formed, spearheaded by veteran umpire Augie Donatelli. The umps wanted an increase in their pension plan, which had been in effect since 1955. An arbiter who retired at age 55 received $200 per year for each year of service. A 10-year ump got a $2,000 annual pension. The umps now wanted $300 per year of service and hired Chicago lawyer John J. Reynolds to represent them.

National League President Warren Giles recommended an increase to $250, but the umps rejected it. At the time, the American League didn't have an umpire association. Its pension plan provided $150 per year until the spring of 1964, when it increased to $250.

The NL umps threatened to strike symbolically on July 4, but nobody wanted it to happen. NL umpire Jocko Conlan contacted Dodgers General Manager Buzzie Bavasi and suggested the umpire's and baseball's representatives hammer out a settlement during the All-Star break. Both sides reached a peaceful agreement.

1968

The ruckus started when two American League umps - Al Salerno and Bill Valentine - were fired without notice by league President Joe Cronin. The umps claimed they were sacrificed for trying to organize a union, and indeed their dismissal came three days after they had mailed letters to fellow umpires about mobilizing. Cronin said, "They are lousy umpires. That's all."

But that wasn't all. The September 16, 1968, firing was only the beginning. A few days earlier, Salerno and Valentine had traveled to Chicago to meet with National League umps about organizing into one union. Valentine said a group of umpires had met with Cronin in 1966 to improve conditions and Cronin "... stormed and raged," according to the arbiter.

The major issue for AL umpires revolved around equal pay for umps in both leagues. Valentine stated the National League scale was $3,500-7,000 higher, depending on experience. Also, per diem allowances were higher in the National League.

In October, 1968, National League umpires voted to join forces with the AL, forming the Major League Umpires Association. Their first joint action was to threaten to strike in 1969 if Salerno and Valentine weren't reinstated. The umpires first threatened to boycott the 1968 World Series, but were dissuaded by Salerno and Valentine.

"We do not wish to deprive baseball fans of their annual classic due to the wrongful conduct of one man (Cronin)," the umpires said in a statement.

The men in blue didn't strike in 1969. In 1970, Salerno and Valentine lost a court battle before the National Labor Relations Board, which ruled there was insufficient evidence to prove Cronin had fired them for union activities.

It had been an ugly court battle. Three AL managers — Alvin Dark of the Indians, Eddie Stanky of the White Sox and Dick Williams of the Red Sox — testified on behalf of the arbiters. Valentine and Salerno were also called to the stand. Valentine broke down when recalling the fateful telephone call from Cronin:

"I told him, 'All of the sudden, after six years in the league, I'm a bad umpire.' He said, 'You've always been a bad umpire.' "

The verdict shocked the umpires. Salerno had rejected four offers of reinstatement including one for an annual salary of $20,000, which was $8,000 more than he was earning when he was fired. The details of the arrangement called for the fired umps to start the 1970 season in the minors, then to be automatically reinstated at mid-season and to receive benefits retroactive to the date of their dismissal.

Salerno held out for more. He wanted $50,000. His attorney, Joe Kelner, was confident of victory with the NLRB and thought they could get $250,000 for each ump on a defamation of character charge. In the end, Salerno gained little except the satisfaction of knowing he and Valentine helped the union get on its feet.

1970

For the first time, umpires walked off the job. The 52-member union voted 37-12 with three abstentions to sit out the National and American League playoffs. The issue was post-season pay, and the umps won a quick victory. Replacement umps were needed for only the first game of each series — Pittsburgh against Cincinnati and Baltimore against Minnesota.

The umpires made a commotion in Pittsburgh, a strong union town. Harry Wendelstedt, president of the union, led a media-opportunity umpire picket line outside Three Rivers Stadium. AL umps in Minnesota just stayed in their hotel rooms.

After one day of minor league replacements, a settlement was reached. The pay scale for the playoffs was raised from $2,500 to $3,000, the World Series climbed from $6,500 to $7,500, then to $8,000 for 1972 and 1973. All-Star Game bonuses were doubled to $1,000.

1978-1979

Umpires voted in a new labor leader, Richie Phillips, who had scored a new contract for NBA officials the previous year. Phillips unveiled his list of demands for umpires: three, one-week vacations during the season; job security after three years' experience for those maintaining a 90 percent rating; cost of living pay increases; a raise in the per diem allowance; first class air transportation and extra pay for working in excess of 162 games.

Baseball was reluctant to negotiate. The umpires had a contract that was in force through 1981, but Phillips contended the demands dealt with areas not covered by the contract.

AL President Lee MacPhail was furious. "We have a valid agreement. It's complete. It has a no-strike clause. We don't think we should be forced to negotiate by the threat of a strike. We have no obligation to reopen the talks."

Phillips begged to differ. In August, umpires staged a one-day strike. Phillips emphasized that an NBA referee with 10 years experience was earning $42,000 compared to $31,000 for a 10-year umpire. U.S. District Court Judge Joseph L. McGlynn Jr., in Philadelphia, issued a temporary restraining order to end the walkout. But the matter was far from over.

The 1979 spring training camps opened without regular umpires. The regular season opened with only two umpires, Paul Pryor of the National League and Ted Hendry of the AL, who had signed contracts. The money issue was critical, and umpires were winning the battle of public sympathy. They wanted to know how baseball could pay George Foster $750,000 a year, but not come up with an extra $15 per diem for the umpires? Stories like the one told by umpire Bill Kunkel resonated with working Americans.

"I get $52 a day for expenses, and my hotel room costs about $26," Kunkel said. "My salary in 1978 was $31,000, and I figure I spent $5,000 out of my own pocket in expenses. I'm on the road 200 days a year. I don't get to see my family except when they come on the road. It's tough."

Umpires who walked picket lines were joined by union workers in Cincinnati, and by NBA referees in New York. In Pittsburgh, attendance dropped. More than 600,000 union workers in Boston vowed not to attend Red Sox games. Umpire unions in Cleveland and San Diego said they would stop cooperating with baseball to provide umpires.

The game was in the hands of college umpires and former professionals. Baseball officials praised their effort, but managers and coaches knew better. They wanted the real thing. Finally, in mid-May, baseball broke and agreed to nearly all of the umpires' demands. The salary range jumped from $22,000 for a second-year ump to a high of $50,000 after 20 years. The per diem allowance increased to $67, rising to $77 in 1981. Post-season assignments were worth more. Umps were allowed paid time off during the season.

But the umps lost one major issue: Baseball retained the right to promote the replacement umps from the minor leagues. They were branded as "scabs" by the rank and file, and suffered more than the usual share of rookie umpire abuse. Umps like Fred Brocklander, who joined the NL staff when the regulars walked out, became an invisible man on his crew. He traveled and ate alone. Replacement umpires became derisively known to veterans as the "Class of 1979."

Steve Fields was a replacement ump. He became the first to lose his job when he was fired in 1982. The National League said he was the lowest rated ump. Fields claimed he was sacrificed. He also shed light on what he and the other seven replacements were going through.

"Once, when I was stepping onto a plane in Houston, the rest of the crew saw me, turned around and took another flight," Fields told *The Washington Post.* "I wouldn't lower myself to these guys' level, I swallowed so much …

"In Cincinnati last season, I was hit on the chin with a foul ball that required seven stitches. But none of the other umps would take my place. They just let me stand there for three hours and bleed. Every inning, I'd go into the Reds dugout and their trainer would put on butterfly stitches and patches, because by sweating and moving my jaw yelling out balls and strikes, it would all just bust open and I would bleed like a stuck pig."

The union demonstrated the power of the Association during the 1979 battle. Although the umpires emerged victorious, baseball may have come out ahead in the long run. Sure, the strike caused problems. The quality of officiating suffered. But the games went on. Overall attendance exceeded the previous year, and baseball seemed prepared to carry on with substitutes. These lessons would prove valuable to baseball in the years to come.

A year later, NL umpire John Kibler summed up the feelings of many of his comrades in an interview with *The Chicago Tribune.*

"Back in 1976, when we were trying to negotiate for ourselves, Lee MacPhail spoke to us. That was when the Andy Messersmith decision had created this free-agent mess, and MacPhail says to us, 'Fellas, we know you deserve more, we know you should have more benefits. But right now, our clubs are broke. There's just no more money in the till for the umpires because of the free-agent thing. Bear with us; it'll be over soon.'

"Broke! Do you know how much money these owners have spent on ballplayers since 1976? Millions? Billions? Zillions? But we ask them for $20, and they tell us to get lost. But it's not only us. The coaches and scouts don't get what they deserve, either. Or the secretaries or anybody. The Phillies owner told his office staff there would be no raises for three years, and Philadelphia has the highest payroll in baseball.

"What they're doing is funneling all the money into one area — ballplayers' salaries. And it's wrong. I can't say what the fair share for the umpires would be, because they won't let me look at the books. But I know we're not getting it. No way. I mean, does it really matter whether a player gets $4.1 million instead of $4.2? Does it?"

Hmm ... I wonder what Kibler would say about Kevin Brown's $112 million contract with the Dodgers?

1982

A settlement on a new contract was reached just before the 1982 openers that called for a new base salary of $26,000, peaking at $75,000 in 1985. Per diem rose from $77 to $90, with cost of living expenses built in. Pension and insurance plans were upgraded. Post-season umpires previously were chosen by rotation, and when baseball wanted to change to a merit selection process, the umpires agreed. They viewed the extra income as compensation for that concession.

1984

The league championship series approached, and umpires wanted an improved post-season financial package. Umps were currently paid $10,000 for the playoffs and $15,000 for the World Series, a total package of $210,000. Umpires asked for a total package of $465,000 and a change in the distribution process. The umps wanted the money to be divided equally among all men in blue, not just the umpires working the games.

The playoffs started with substitutes. A crew of four, instead of the usual six used in the post-season, worked the Cubs-Padres opener. No umps were positioned on the foul lines. In Kansas City, Bill Deegan, retired since 1980, was behind the plate for the first two games of the Royals-Tigers championship series. The AL used six umpires.

The umpires ended the strike in time for NL officials to work the fifth and final game of the Cubs-Padres series. Both sides agreed to allow Commissioner Peter Ueberroth, who had replaced

Bowie Kuhn only seven days earlier, to arbitrate their dispute.

The umpires had found a friend. Ueberroth awarded them a package worth almost $1.4 million over the next three years. He agreed that a pool should be established for post-season earnings and raised the total income to $405,000. By 1986, it went to $465,000. Also, World Series, playoff and All-Star Game umpires returned to a rotation selection.

"Umpires are an integral part of Major League Baseball," Ueberroth said. "They are important to the players, fans and all of organized baseball. These 60 men are the best in their profession. They have paid their dues with many years of hard work and training in amateur baseball and the minor leagues. They should be recognized accordingly."

1985

Former President Richard Nixon, an avid baseball fan, was selected to arbitrate the latest contract dispute that centered on the expanded playoff schedule. When umpires agreed to their 1984 deal, playoffs were a best-of-five series. In 1985, playoffs switched to a best-of-seven format. Umpires threatened to work only the first five games, but they agreed to stay on the job when the parties agreed to binding arbitration.

Nixon found in favor of the umpires and granted a 40 percent increase in post-season pay.

1987

Umpires reached an agreement 2 1/2 hours before the opening pitch of the season. The new salary range was $40,000 for rookies to $100,000 for 20-year veterans, and a new per diem of $148. The post-season pool was increased from $641,000 to $800,000.

1990

Umpires refused to work several exhibition games to protest being excluded from participating in the process of revising the regular-season schedule. They also demanded to be paid for the spring training games canceled by the owners' 32-day lockout.

1991

For the sixth time in 21 years, the umpires went on strike two days before the season opener because they faced a management lockout. Amateur umpires called the final two days of spring training, along with seven of the eight Opening Day games.

When the strike was settled, umpires' minimum salary was increased from $41,000 to $60,000. The maximum soared from $105,000 to $175,000. Umps got a third week of in-season vacation, and a rise in per diem from $169 to $185, along with increases in medical benefits, insurance coverage and pensions. The post-season pool increased to $1.2 million.

In exchange, baseball won the right to select umpires for the All-Star Game, playoffs and World Series based on merit.

1995

The most bizarre spring training in history unfolded with college and high school umpires calling exhibition games held with replacement players. With baseball fixed on ending the players' lockout that canceled the 1994 World Series, few noticed the umpires had been locked out since January 1.

Umpires were fortunate not to lose wages in the players' strike that began August 12, 1994. The umps' contract covers them up to 75 missed game days. But when December 31 and the end of the four-year contract passed, the umpires were cut off.

In May, owners settled with umpires and ended the 120-day lockout. Increases included: salaries ballooned from $75,000 to $225,000, up from $60,000-$175,000. All umpires received a post-season bonus of $20,000. Previously, some got $10,000 and some got $20,000, depending on experience.

Bonuses for the All-Star Game rose from $2,500 to $5,000, league championship series bonuses jumped from $5,000 to $15,000, and bonuses for the World Series rose from $5,000 to $17,500. Umps working the new round of playoffs would receive $12,500, with permission to work the World Series the same year.

"Having labor peace with the umpires over the next five years is a welcome and necessary development," said acting commissioner Bud Selig.

Going strong to the hoop

Baseball wasn't Richie Phillips' only game. He also worked for golf officials, and represented the NBA referees association from its inception in 1976. A judge ruled he was illegally fired in 1984, after a 4-1 vote by the executive board. Referees had voted 18-10 to remove Phillips.

The action came after a contentious 1983-84 season, which opened without the refs. Their three-year contract expired September 1; they were locked out after the union's refusal to give the NBA a no-strike pledge. The lockout lasted 100 days.

The settlement provided for a base salary of $28,000 for rookies, up to $85,000 for those with 16 years in the league. After three years, the scale increased from $28,000 to $90,000. In 1982, the lowest paid official had made $18,000.

Substitute referees from colleges and the CBA called games inside arenas while locked-out officials picketed outside. One referee returned from the previous season, Officials Supervisor Darell Garretson, who wasn't a Phillips fan. "I figured this would go on until Richie Phillips got his picture on national TV and X amount of newsprint," Garretson said during the lockout. "You see, he'll make X amount of money from the negotiations, so it'll go on until he feels he's reached that plateau."

Strikes were threatened when contracts ended in 1977 and 1980, with officials walking off the job at the end of the 1977 regular season. Substitute officials, along with holdouts Richie Powers and Earl Strom, worked the opening round of the playoffs. The refs returned after agreeing to a $150 per game increase for the remainder of the playoffs.

STRANGE CALLS

Ump center stage in Merkle's misdeed

For sheer dramatics, no event in baseball's history tops the 1908 Fred Merkle incident, in which an umpire's call changed the course of a season and led to the suicide of his boss.

The hotly-contested National League pennant race among the New York Giants, Cubs and Pirates was in its final days, when Chicago visited New York September 23. The score was 1-1 in the bottom of the ninth, with Giants runners Moose McCormick on third and Merkle on first.

Al Bridwell lined what appeared to be a game-winning single up the middle. As Giants fans rushed onto the field in celebration, Merkle peeled off his route to second base and headed for the clubhouse.

Alert Cubs second baseman Johnny Evers noticed what became known as "Merkle's boner." He called for the ball from center fielder Artie Hofman, who threw the ball back to the infield. It sailed past Evers and was caught by Giants coach "Iron Man" Joe McGinnity, who also noticed Merkle's mistake.

McGinnity soon became overpowered by Cubs now wise to the

situation, and heaved the ball into a crowd of fans behind third base. Several Cubs players followed the ball and Joe Tinker came away with it. He tossed it to Evers, who was standing on second base.

Umpire Hank O'Day had not left the field. Frank Chance got in O'Day's face, claiming Merkle was out for not touching second. Because it was a force out, McCormick's run didn't count, leaving the score tied. A mob soon surrounded the player and ump, although, as *The New York Herald* reported, most fans weren't alert to the controversy. They merely seized an opportunity to take shots at an arbiter: "Those within reach began pounding him on all available parts not covered by the protector, while the unfortunate attackers on the outskirts began sending messages by way of cushions, newspapers and other missiles."

O'Day didn't render his decision immediately. However, while the ump was in the dressing room, O'Day told a reporter Merkle didn't touch second, the run didn't count and he would speak with National League President Harry Pulliam about the decision.

Merkle said he touched second; not on his original route, but after he saw what the Cubs were doing. Giants pitcher Christy Mathewson, one of the most respected players in the game's history, said he saw Merkle touch the bag. Bob Emsile, the umpire on the bases, said he didn't see the play, because he was trying to avoid the onslaught of fans rushing onto the field. In the meantime, O'Day had sprinted from his location at home plate to the mound, which put him in the best position to rule on the play.

A week later, the Cubs claimed a victory by forfeit because they showed up at the Polo Grounds early the next day to finish the game, but the Giants did not. Pulliam stood by O'Day's account and issued this statement:

"As much as I deplore the unfortunate ending of a brilliantly played game, as well as the subsequent controversy, I have no alternative but to be guided by law. I believe in sportsmanship, but would it be good sportsmanship to repudiate my umpires simply to condone the undisputed blunder of a player? The playing rules say the decision of an arbiter on a question of fact is final. This whole controversy hinges on a simple question: Was Merkle forced out at second base? Umpire-in-chief O'Day says he was. O'Day is no novice … As an umpire, he ranks second to none; his integrity has never been questioned."

The controversy would have ended had the Giants hung on to win the pennant. They did not. The Giants and Cubs finished the season with 98-55 records, with Pittsburgh merely a half-game behind. The first playoff in the National League would settle the matter. A talented young umpire, Bill Klem, was assigned to call the balls and strikes. The Cubs won 4-2.

The postscripts ran the gamut. The Cubs went on to defeat the Tigers in the World Series, but haven't won a championship since. In a subsequent meeting, the National League owners (with those from New York and Chicago abstaining), commended O'Day for his actions. Merkle was 19 years old and in his second season at the time. He went on to play 16 seasons, primarily as a first baseman, including three years with the Cubs.

Pulliam lost his battle with depression over the controversy and July 19, 1909, committed suicide.

Pine tar and feathered

July 24, 1983, the Royals George Brett stepped up to the plate against the Yankees Goose Gossage in Yankee Stadium. It was the top of the ninth, New York led 4-3 and Kansas City had a runner on.

Whack! Just like he did three years earlier in the American League playoffs, Brett hammered the Gossage offering over the right-field wall. Immediately after Brett crossed home plate, Yankees manager Billy Martin shot out of the dugout. Martin complained to home plate umpire, Tim McClelland, that the pine tar on Brett's bat extended too far up the barrel, in violation of a rule intended to keep baseballs clean.

"I'm standing on the second step of the dugout, looking back over my shoulder," Brett wrote in his autobiography, *Last of a Breed.* "I said, 'That's so much bullshit. If they call me out, I'm going to kill one of them. I swear to God, I'll kill 'em.'

"I no sooner got those words out of my mouth, than (McClelland) calls me out. I went crazy. I don't really remember everything that happened. It was one of the few times in my life where I actually snapped and I had no idea what I was doing. I had to see the replays."

McClelland, a rookie umpire, had to be protected from an

onrushing Brett by crew chief Joe Brinkman. McClelland had reached his decision by placing the bat across home plate, which measures 17 inches. The pine tar limit is 18 inches from the knob.

The Royals protested to AL President Lee MacPhail, who upheld the protest because Brett had not violated the spirit of the rule. Not since that game has a baseball protest been upheld. Legal challenges from fans and boycott threats from New York players never materialized, and August 18, the game resumed. Martin didn't take it seriously. He put pitcher Ron Guidry in center field, left-hander Don Mattingly at second base, and sent Roy Smalley to the plate in the bottom of the ninth with pine tar covering the bat.

As play resumed, Martin ordered his pitcher, George Frazier, to throw the ball to each base, claiming Brett and the base-runner, U.L. Washington, had not touched all the bases. But the American League was prepared. The crew chief of the umpires, Dave Phillips, produced a notarized letter stating Brett and Washington had touched all the bases.

"With all that happened afterward, what got lost was the pitch George hit," Gossage said. "It almost hit him in the ear, but he tomahawked the thing over the right-field fence. It was unbelievable that he could hit that ball."

Call keeps Royals' hopes alive

The 1985 World Series lives in infamy in St. Louis. The Cardinals, ahead three games to two, entered the bottom of the ninth inning of Game Six, leading 1-0. What happened next was arguably the most controversial call in World Series history.

The Royals Jorge Orta led off the ninth with an infield tap to the right side. First baseman Jack Clark fielded the ball and tossed to pitcher Todd Worrell, who was covering the bag. Orta appeared out by a half-step, but umpire Don Denkinger called him safe. Cardinals manager Whitey Herzog argued, saying the only way he could imagine Orta being safe was if Worrell had come off the bag. Denkinger, after the game, said that wasn't the case.

"It was a bang-bang play," Denkinger said. "In that situation, I try to watch the foot and the ball. In my judgment, the runner was on first base before the catch, so I called him safe."

The Royals went on to score two runs for the victory, and won the seventh game in a rout. The miscalled play rekindled the rotation vs. merit debate of selecting umpires.

"Because the two best teams are in the World Series, I think you ought to have the best umpires," Herzog said. "I think it's a disgrace — and Denkinger's a good umpire, by the way."

At the moment, Herzog felt the need to praise Denkinger, who was working home plate for the seventh game. It didn't matter — Herzog got tossed in Kansas City's 11-0 victory.

Yankees kid around

Major league umpires were not in the best of moods for the 1996 American League Championship Series between the Yankees and Orioles. Baltimore second baseman Roberto Alomar was still playing after spitting in the face of John Hirschbeck in the earlier playoff round. Umps wanted Alomar to be suspended, but Alomar's appeal kept him in the lineup.

However, the incident was temporarily forgotten when a bad call in the eighth inning of the opening game at Yankee Stadium transformed a 12-year-old boy into a hometown hero, and reduced a respected arbiter to a victim of scorn.

With Baltimore leading 4-3, Yankees shortstop Derek Jeter smacked a drive deep to right. Orioles outfielder Tony Tarasco, with his back to the wall, appeared to have a play on the ball. But reaching over the fence was Jeff Maier, who knocked the ball into the stands with his glove. Umpire Richie Garcia, who was working the right-field line, ruled home run. That tied the game, and New York won in 11 innings. The Yankees went on to win the series in five games.

Maier became a mini-celebrity and appeared on talk shows, including *Good Morning America*. Garcia couldn't have felt worse. He described the play to *Referee* magazine:

"After seeing the flight of the ball, I looked at the fielder, which is routinely what we do. I saw (Tarasco's) glove up against the wall. I've seen it a hundred times on replay. I've seen it a hundred times in my dreams. I'm waiting for the ball to hit his glove or go over the wall or whatever. Suddenly, (Tarasco) jumps and there's no ball. I never saw the kid reach out and hit the ball. My first instinct was, the ball had to be above his glove and it had to be above the fence, so it had to be a home run. There was no doubt in my mind.

"I really didn't see it. That bothered me … I think the biggest argument is whether he would have caught the ball or not. Honestly, I don't think he would have caught the ball. But I don't think the ball would have gone over the fence, either."

After the game, Garcia agreed to face the media. He first looked at a replay and saw he had missed the call. Garcia explained what he saw and didn't see. The series moved to Baltimore, where he was booed vociferously. But Garcia said he'd rather hear that noise than the cheers he received in New York.

VOICES: Steve Palermo

The American League umpiring career of Steve Palermo, which spanned nearly two decades, came to a tragic end July 7, 1991. Palermo and fellow umpire, Richie Garcia, were dining at Campisi's in Dallas after a game. As the restaurant was closing, Palermo looked out the window and saw two waitresses being mugged. Palermo and his group chased the robber and caught him. But as they were holding him down, a car drove by and a gunman shot Palermo, severing his spinal cord. The incident didn't slow Palermo down. Although no longer able to umpire, he worked as an announcer for the Seattle Mariners and New York Yankees, conducted studies for the commissioner's office, and along with his wife, Debbie, founded the Steve Palermo Foundation for Spinal Cord Injuries. Palermo shared his thoughts about the men in blue and the unforgettable summer of 1999.

The bottom line is, a lot of quality people got caught in the crossfire and lost their jobs; that never should have happened.

On one side, you had Major League Baseball talking about making changes that were never actually proposed. On the other side, you had Richie Phillips reacting to that, not really listening to what baseball was saying — just forming his own plans. It turned into one heavy-duty pissing match.

Both sides, Phillips and baseball, want the fired umpires back. Phillips wants them all back, and baseball wants most of them back. Baseball needs them because the game needs quality umpiring.

Phillips gambled with careers. When he got the resignations, I think he should have taken them to baseball, put them on the table and said, "Let's sit down and talk about this." But he submitted them, and that caught a lot of guys off guard.

I don't know how it's going to play out. I think baseball will try to get some umpires back, but baseball can pick and choose. What baseball needs to do is to help the umpires improve. It needs to set up a system so that the game can help them get better.

Umpires are the enforcers of law that baseball legislators pass down. I've always thought the lords of baseball should consult with the people who are on the field every day when they wanted to make changes. They may not get the answers they want to hear, but at least they'll be hearing it from the people who are closest to the game.

When something is fixed, you've got to look at the reasons it mal-functioned in the first place. Baseball talks about changing the strike zone. We tried that seven or eight years ago in spring training. There were complaints, so baseball backed off and nothing was fine-tuned. But the umpires didn't mind doing it.

It's like in 1988, when we called a million balks. The pitchers weren't coming to a complete stop — they were going through a red light. So the American League and the National League put a cop at the intersection. There was a big outcry because of all the balks we called. But umpires were just doing what baseball had asked them to do. The following year, we called only a quarter-million balks. Then, pitchers were retrained. They came to a stop, so we didn't have to call as many balks.

The players' poll was set up to fail. When I watch an umpire work, I offer constructive criticism. I'm not going to tell him he's lousy or he ranks last in my book. If he's a good young ump, he's going to listen and learn. All the veteran umpires today learned something from older umpires when they broke in. I don't know what they planned to do with the information from the survey, but it wasn't construc-tive.

All umpires are different. Some are better than others. Why doesn't every player hit like Tony Gwynn or George Brett? Why doesn't every player copy their stance and swing? There are reasons those guys are two of the best hitters in baseball history, just like there are reasons some umpires are better than others.

There are 64 umpires. I might be the worst of those 64, the very worst. But I'm still better than the best in the minor leagues. It's funny how it works. I may miss a call on the bases for the Red Sox, and make 7,450 calls before I see Boston again. But the next time I see them, they know me as the guy who blew that call on the bases a few weeks ago. They think I'm terrible on the bases. When you get a reputation, it's tough to shake it.

These days, technology is better than ever. Television shows replays from so many angles. Why not use this technology to improve the game? I used to do that. I remember one time I was in the locker room 90 minutes after a game. I called Jose Canseco out on a pitch and he didn't like it. I brought him into a video room and we both watched the replay. We talked about it.

Communication is the key. But this summer, the talking stopped. Baseball didn't talk to the umpires. Some umpires thought Richie Phillips wasn't communicating with them. Because of that, 22 men lost their jobs. That didn't have to happen.

FOOTBALL

OFFICIALLY SPEAKING

Wake-up calls

The 1998 NFL season unfolded with the usual crazy bounces. The Vikings and Broncos established superiority. The Falcons and Cardinals were surprisingly good. Heralded rookie quarterbacks Peyton Manning and Ryan Leaf took their early lumps, although Manning recovered nicely. Veteran quarterbacks Randall Cunningham and Doug Flutie dipped into the fountain of youth. Randy Moss got jaw-droppingly better every week.

The games, teams and players were the focus, as it should be. Oh, there was the occasional blunder by officials, protested by the losing coach, who was angered by a blown call that kept alive the other team's winning drive or negated his touchdown. Probably the loudest protest came after an October 18 game between the 49ers and Colts in Indianapolis.

Colts coach Jim Mora blew a gasket when two pass interference calls went against his team and wiped out turnovers. The calls kept alive a San Francisco touchdown drive late in the second quarter, and the 49ers won the game by a field goal. The NFL office made a rare apology to the Colts the following week. Former 49ers coach Bill Walsh, threw in his two cents' worth in an article for *The Sporting News.* " … I knew exactly how he felt. No coach deserves to have a bad call cost his team a game …"

Little did Walsh or anyone else know, Mora's problems would be largely forgotten in the next few weeks.

A handful of other controversial calls found their way into postgame highlights and statements by coaches. The use of instant replay to settle disputes, not used by the NFL since 1991, was collecting proponents, but there was no real groundswell. Replay seemed no closer to reality by Thanksgiving than when the season started. But what happened next became the NFL story of the season, and the football officiating story of the century.

A sequence of events over an 11-day period pushed NFL officials squarely into the public eye. Controversial calls in Pontiac, Foxboro and East Rutherford that coincidentally favored the home teams triggered an outcry not only from the bitter losing teams, but from fans nationwide. By mid-December, officials could do nothing right in the public's view.

It all started with the flip of a coin.

The Steelers appeared to benefit from close calls throughout most of their Thanksgiving Day game at Detroit. Quarterback Kordell Stewart may have gotten away with a fumble, and a Lions interception was nullified when officials ruled the ball had hit the turf first. Regulation play ended 16-16, and team representatives headed to midfield for the coin toss.

Referee Phil Luckett, an eight-year veteran in his second season as crew chief, performed the duty. As the visiting team, the Steelers made the call while the coin was in the air. The voice of running back Jerome Bettis wasn't clear as he made his call. "Tails," is what he claimed to have said.

"When (Luckett) flipped the coin, it almost hit him," Bettis said after the game. "He jumped away from it and I have to believe that caused him to forget what I said, but I said tails, clear as day."

Luckett heard it differently. "He called heads, tails," Luckett told a pool reporter in a postgame interview. "When it hit the ground, it bounced to tails. I said, 'You called heads, so Detroit has won the toss.' "

Safety Carnell Lake, standing next to Bettis, also tried to inform Luckett that he was wrong. "I put my reputation on it," Lake said. "(Bettis) called tails. I've never seen anything as blatant as that. I even looked at the Lions and they're like, 'Wow.' They obviously didn't say anything because they wanted the football."

The toss wasn't replayed, although under NFL rules, it could have been if Luckett determined there were sufficient grounds. The toss stood. The Lions took the kickoff and drove 41 yards in seven plays to set up Jason Hanson's 42-yard game-winning field goal. Steelers coach Bill Cowher was outraged.

"What makes me mad is you fight, you scratch for 60 minutes, then the game is decided by people that wear the striped shirts," he said. "There's something wrong with that."

In a previous season, Cowher stuffed a photograph into the shirt pocket of an official at halftime to prove the officials erroneously penalized his team for having too many men on the field.

The flap had a stage all to itself. The game was one of only two that day, a Thanksgiving tradition, and the only one broadcast by CBS. Instead of competing for attention with 13 other games, Pittsburgh-Detroit and the coin flip stood practically alone for media dissection. There was plenty of time to run through the scoring highlights ad nauseum and turn the coin flip into the biggest controversy of the season.

As a practical matter, the NFL changed the coin flip policy before the following week's games. The new policy stated the visiting captain was required to make the call before the flip. Also, the back judge and field judge would stand next to the captains to eliminate confusion. But the changes did little to soothe the Steelers, whose record fell to 7-5. Even Lions owner William Clay Ford vented about those earlier calls that went against his team.

"If you beat the Steelers and the referee, that's pretty good for one day," Ford told *The Detroit Free Press.* "I've never seen a game called like that in my life. I thought it was terrible. I don't give a (bleep) if the commissioner fines me or not. It's just terrible. If we don't get instant replay, I give up … The biggest turkey out there was wearing a striped shirt and white hat."

As for the coin flip, Ford wasn't willing to give Luckett's crew the benefit of the doubt. "The officials screwed up everything else," he said. "Why shouldn't we think they screwed that up, too?"

Everyone chuckled that Sunday when Falcons coach Dan Reeves sent captain Jesse Tuggle to the coin flip before their game at St. Louis with a handmade sign that read "HEADS." In the Bears-Bucs game, Chicago captain Marty Carter joked that he heard "heads" after Tampa Bay won the toss with a "tails" call.

Luckett wasn't laughing. He was steaming, because he knew he had followed the rulebook and made the correct call. But no one was supporting him. No word came from the NFL office, perhaps because there would be more controversy involving playoff hopeful teams four days later.

"We got robbed"

At Foxboro, the Bills and Patriots battled to a final play that should never have happened, according to the Bills. The outcome of the game prompted Buffalo owner Ralph Wilson, an instant replay opponent, to reverse his stance.

The Patriots trailed 21-17. On its final drive, New England faced a fourth and nine from the Buffalo 36. Patriots quarterback Drew Bledsoe fired a sideline pass to wide receiver Shawn Jefferson, who had run his route 10 yards, enough for the first down.

Jefferson had lifted his left foot just before the ball arrived, and his right foot was in the air. When he gained control of the ball and came down, he was obviously out of bounds. But line judge Dave Anderson, who had a clear view of the play, spotted the ball on the 26. He conferred with field judge Dick Creed, and the play stood.

The Bills couldn't believe it. Not only did they think the catch was illegal, but there was the matter of the spot. They claimed Jefferson stepped out of bounds closer to the 27, which might have prevented a first down and ended New England's possession. They didn't get that call, either.

The crusher came on what should have been the final snap. The play started from the 26 with six seconds remaining. The Patriots lined up three wideouts on the left side — Jefferson on the outside, Tony Simmons on the inside and Terry Glenn behind them. Bledsoe launched the Hail Mary. When the ball reached the end zone, Glenn jumped for it and Buffalo strong safety, Henry Jones, made contact. The ball hit Glenn in the chest and bounced away.

On a Hail Mary, with so many bodies gravitating toward one spot, anything less than a blatant shove is rarely called pass interference. But that's what first-year side judge Terry McAuley called against Jones. The Patriots were given a final play from the 1. Bledsoe lobbed a pass to Ben Coates in the back of the end zone for the touchdown. The Patriots tacked on a two-point conversion after the Bills had left for the locker room, for a 25-21 victory.

Under the old instant replay rules, Jefferson's pass reception at the 26 probably wouldn't have held up. Without instant replay, the call was not correctable. Had Jefferson been ruled out of bounds, Buffalo would have taken possession and the Hail Mary wouldn't have happened. Instead of forging a three-way tie with

Miami and the Jets with an 8-4 record, Buffalo fell to 7-5, the same record as New England. Wilson and the Bills couldn't believe what they had seen. "We got robbed," Wilson said. "It was awful. I've been watching football for six decades. Pass interference. What was that?"

Bills defensive end Bruce Smith called it "... the most frustrating loss I've experienced in 14 years." Writers covering the game pointed out the officiating crew, with one exception, was the same that had worked the controversial Colts-49ers game that produced an apology.

There was no apology after the Patriots-Bills game, only a fax from Commissioner Paul Tagliabue informing Wilson that he was subject to a $50,000 fine for criticizing the officials. Wilson responded with a statement of his own: "I described two calls, back-to-back, as probably the worst I have witnessed in the 60 years I have watched pro football. Those two calls cost the Bills a very important game, one in which our team fought back courageously from a substantial deficit.

"Society today is more enlightened. Fair comment and criticism are rampant. The entire media as a unit is frank and the millions watching a game are frank.

"But the commissioner lecturing to me as if I were a novice, instead of one who has been involved in football infinitely longer than he has, contends that criticizing a call has 'destructive and corrosive effects on the game.'

"Which is more destructive and corrosive — errant calls in front of millions of viewers or my statements of opinion? People all over the country registered shock at the way the officials, however honorable their purpose, took the game away from us. Even the league has admitted the calls near the conclusion of the game were incorrect.

"Monday morning, the commissioner can sermonize on destruction and corrosion, but he has never experienced the pain of blowing a crucial game due to officiating. I have yet to decide whether I will pay or challenge the fine.

"But, at age 80, I don't need pompous lectures from the commissioner, and I feel that the $50,000 fine is not only unwarranted, but punitive in nature. The next time, he may ask me to sit in a corner."

"God's a Jets Fan"

The trifecta of controversy was completed the following weekend, when the Seahawks visited the New York Jets. Coach Bill Parcell's Jets were rolling along with an 8-4 record. Seattle, which hadn't made the playoffs in coach Dennis Erickson's previous three seasons, were 6-6 and in desperate need of an upset victory to spark a season-ending rally. Erickson's job was on the line.

The Seahawks charged to a 31-25 lead and victory seemed assured. The Jets were facing a fourth-and-goal on the 5. With 27 seconds remaining, quarterback Vinny Testaverde opted to keep the ball. He found a seam, lunged forward and went down just before crossing the goal line. There was no call, which at the moment, seemed like the correct call.

Then the arms went up. Touchdown. The 72,000 at the Meadowlands roared their approval. The Seahawks went nuts. The replay from every television angle indicated the ball and most of Testaverde's body fell short of the goal line. The call was made by head linesman Earnie Frantz, part of Luckett's crew working the game.

The New York tabloids had a field day on Monday.

"God's a Jets Fan," screamed *The New York Post.*

"Vinny falls short on Jets final chance, but refs say it's CLOSE ENOUGH," blared *The Daily News.*

The loss all but eliminated the Seahawks from the playoffs. The next day, Erickson received a call from NFL Officials Supervisor, Jerry Seeman, who attempted to explain the call. After receiving the game report from the officiating crew, Seeman told Erickson Frantz confused Testaverde's white helmet with the ball. Erickson held his tongue and didn't publicly criticize the officials. The Seahawks didn't reach the playoffs and Erickson was fired after the season.

Any one of the three calls earlier in the season would have created a minor furor, much like the Colts-49ers game. But the timing and conditions couldn't have been worse for a league that cares deeply about public perception. The NFL is a financial bonanza, the leading corporate giant among American sport leagues. Hits to its image are taken seriously, and the NFL had just taken three major blows. Later, one of the calls was proven correct.

Unquestionably correct. But that didn't help the NFL in late 1998, when confidence in officials reached an all-time low.

Polls by ESPN, CNN-SI and Fox indicated more than 90 percent of fans favored use of instant replay to sort out the mess. Hysteria from Buffalo and Pittsburgh, where fans believed their teams had been victimized by poor officiating, was expected. But national publications were now taking notice. *Newsweek* weighed in on the controversies. *USA Today* gave it front-page play. Richard Sandomir, who writes about sports and television for *The New York Times* said, "It has become abundantly clear there are a dozen key calls a fan could point out over the course of a season that could use another look. Not having replay creates a lot of negative talk. I think bringing back replay would create more talk, more positive talk."

The most revealing piece was provided by Peter King in a *Sports Illustrated* article December 14. King was granted access to a meeting of officials who were reviewing the previous week's game film, a collection of highlights from around the league provided by the NFL office with Seeman's voice-over critique. The end of the tape showed the two plays from the Bills-Patriots game. Seeman said the officials were incorrect, that Jefferson didn't have both feet down in bounds.

The next highlight on the tape was the Hail Mary pass interference call, with this rebuke from Seeman: "We don't want to determine the outcome of games unless it's the most blatant thing you've seen. There is no foul. It's incomprehensible, as much as we prepare ... When we make such a blatant error in judgment, we deserve the criticism we get. The greatest attribute of the NFL official is common sense. Under no conditions should an official or officials ever be involved in a situation like this again."

Playoff headaches

The final three weekends of the regular season passed without major incident, and the NFL hoped for a controversy-free post-season. Fat chance.

Buffalo, in the playoffs despite the loss at New England, traveled to Miami for a wild-card game. The Bills trailed, 24-14, and drove deep into Dolphins territory. Wide receiver Andre Reed caught a pass and tried to lunge over the goal line. He was ruled down inside the 1. Reed jumped up, bumped into field judge Steve Zimmer and was ejected. The Bills were penalized 15 yards and settled for a field goal in a 24-17 loss. A month earlier, Bills owner Ralph Wilson fired the shots. This time, the entire Buffalo team pulled the trigger.

"I've never seen officiating this bad," said guard Ruben Brown.

"I don't know if they have other jobs, but I think they need to devote full time to what they do," Reed said. "Some of the calls they made this year were the worst in 20 years."

"I think they should get rid of all of them," running back Thurman Thomas said.

Turns out, the officials spotted the ball correctly on Reed's reception, and Reed did himself in by jumping into Zimmer. Reed later said he didn't bump Zimmer purposely, but was caught up in the emotions of the moment.

The following day on the West Coast, more wild-card controversy erupted. The Packers prematurely began celebrating a victory over the 49ers. Green Bay led, 27-23, and thought they had clinched the game on a fumble recovery. Jerry Rice had caught his first pass of the game, a six-yarder on second-and-10 from the Packers 47 with 40 seconds remaining. Green Bay linebacker Bernardo Harris and rookie nickel back Scott McGarrahan stripped the ball, and Harris recovered.

But line judge Jeff Bergman ruled that Rice didn't fumble and field judge Kevin Mack, who had a better view, didn't overrule Bergman. Four plays later, Steve Young fired a game-winning 25-yard touchdown pass to Terrell Owens. Another team screamed injustice.

"That was clearly a fumble," Packers General Manager Ron Wolf said. "We clearly recovered. The game's over. It's tough to lose, no matter how you do it. But when you make a play in a championship game and it's not awarded to you, there's something wrong with the whole system."

The irony couldn't be avoided. Packers coach Mike Holmgren was the co-chair of the NFL's competition committee, which had killed the idea of using instant replay for the playoffs. After the three controversial calls of the regular season, the committee floated a proposal that would give each team two challenges at the discretion of the zebra during the last two minutes of a game, and the decision would be made by the referee looking at a sideline monitor. It also would allow a coach who is out of challenges in the final two minutes to make a challenge, with the referee's consent.

But the measure lost by a 7-1 vote. Holmgren, a replay advocate, voted "no" this time. Opponents didn't want to appear to be bowing to public pressure by changing the rules that had been in place for the regular season.

There would be one more major playoff controversy to deal with. By the time the 49ers and Falcons met in the conference semifinal, officials were under siege. Every questionable call became a full-blown controversy. Case in point — San Francisco running back Terry Kirby recovered his own fumble instead of Atlanta's Chuck Smith, who returned it 46 yards for a touchdown. The home fans in the Georgia Dome went nuts. TV analysts went nuts. Smith seemingly had given the Falcons a 21-0 lead. But no touchdown signal was given. After a lengthy discussion, officials said Smith recovered the fumble and was down by contact. However, upon further review, they switched versions, ruling Kirby recovered and was down by contact.

Replays appeared to support the officials. But they were not given the benefit of the doubt at that moment — not after the previous weeks of controversy.

My mistake

Of the three major questionable calls during that 11-day stretch, one was not a blunder. Thanks to an enhanced audio tape of the coin toss and a conversation between Luckett and Cowher, there was no doubt Luckett acted properly. An article appeared in the May issue of *Referee* magazine affirming Luckett's written report to the NFL following the game. Luckett's version was supported by a tape from a Pittsburgh television station that recorded Bettis saying, "Heads, tails." Immediately after the toss, Luckett went to Cowher and explained what had just transpired. Bettis is heard admitting to his coach that he said, "Hea-tails." Under NFL rules, Luckett accepted Bettis' first utterance, which was "heads," or enough of the word to make a reasonable assumption that heads was Bettis' choice.

Columnist Bob Smizik of the *Pittsburgh Post-Gazette* wrote an apology column and ended by imploring others to follow: "Well, turns out the hapless buffoons in this story are the media members, including this reporter, players, coaches and owners who ridiculed Luckett that day and for weeks afterward. Also included on this dubious list is the National Football League, which denied Luckett a playoff assignment because of the coin-toss call."

Had this information been widely circulated within a few days of the call, Luckett's reputation might have been salvaged. As it was, after the Jets-Seahawks debacle worked by Luckett's crew, the fans believed the same guy who blew the coin toss was now on the hook for the bad spot on the Testaverde touchdown, which was a call Luckett didn't make. Luckett was right about the coin toss and wasn't directly involved in the call of Testaverde's touchdown, yet he unfairly became the poster child for the ills of NFL officiating. That's why he took his case to *Referee*.

"I was supported personally, but regrettably, I felt no support publicly," Luckett said. "I don't feel the NFL handled it well. Perhaps they thought it would go away quickly. Unfortunately, it did not."

Those incidents cost Luckett a spot in post-season play, although he was given playoff pay of $9,800, and an admission that the NFL believed their official had acted properly. However, the NFL did not assign Luckett to work the playoffs because it feared more public relations hits if Luckett worked a game. "Not assigning me to a playoff game told everyone I messed up this year," Luckett said.

In the final analysis, the officials and especially Luckett didn't mess up as badly as was originally thought. The missed out-of-bounds call on the pass reception in the Patriots-Bills game, and the Testaverde touchdown against the Seahawks were blunders that instant replay could have rectified.

The mistakes aren't to be underestimated or excused. They harmed teams in the post-season. Seattle would have made the playoffs with a victory over the Jets. The Patriots would not have — they would have missed post-season play if Buffalo had defeated them, and the Bills would have had home field advantage instead of traveling to Miami.

The league breathed a collective sigh of relief when the conference championships and Super Bowl passed with no obvious officiating mistakes. But the momentum for instant replay, voted down at every opportunity since 1991 (except as an experiment for a few preseason games in 1996), had clearly shifted and was headed for a resounding victory at the NFL meetings in March.

THE LIFE AND TIMES OF INSTANT REPLAY

"Didn't they just do that?"

Ebbets Field, better known for its baseball tenant, was the site of football's first televised game October 22, 1939. The Philadelphia Eagles met the Brooklyn Dodgers before 13,000 fans. Most of the players were not aware of the TV cameras pointed at them. The broadcast, over New York's W2XBS, was received by about 1,000 homes.

Television recorded another first December 7, 1963, when CBS debuted its new toy, the instant replay, during the Army-Navy game from Philadelphia. Initially, viewers were confused. Fans of the Midshipmen marveled at how Roger Staubach could complete a 10-yarder, then throw the exact same pass a moment later.

To players, coaches and fans, there was an obvious use for the invention beyond the entertainment value. Naturally, a controversial call accelerated the drumbeat. Washingtonians won't soon forget November 16, 1975. In a critical division game, the Redskins led the St. Louis Cardinals, 17-10, in the final minute. Cards quarterback Jim Ray Hart connected with Mel Gray, who made a sensational catch at the goal line to set up the tying touchdown. But the ball was knocked from Gray's hands by a defender. Officials ruled Gray had the ball long enough for a touchdown, and St. Louis won in overtime.

Talk about political posturing — Congressmen, smitten with the recent success of coach George Allen's Redskins, were outraged. A local attorney filed suit in federal court to reverse the decision. Allen may have been as "old school" as anybody in the game, but not surprisingly, he favored technology in the heat of this moment.

"I think there should be a rule that states, when something like this comes up, when a bad decision is made, a team doesn't have to suffer for it," Allen said.

Before the end of the regular season, the 26 NFL coaches were polled by a video production company. More than half said they favored instant replay to determine close calls. An official vote was not called at that time, but the futuristic opinions of coaches nearly a quarter-century ago are interesting to note.

Lions coach Rick Forzano was a no-vote, stating, "Part of the fun of being in athletics is judgement calls. Maybe in the future it will become so technical, you won't need officials or coaches. You'll have machines out there."

The Chiefs Hank Stram advanced a can-of-worms theory: "You might see holding that you originally didn't see while you were looking at the replay of another penalty. It would just open up another can of worms."

Three years later, the NFL conducted a study and concluded instant replay wouldn't eliminate enough controversy to make it worthwhile. Too much expense and delay made it impractical. But by 1980, most coaches thought it was only a matter of time. "Somewhere down the line, it's going to come," the Rams Ray Malavasi said. "If you have the sophistication of television, why not use it?"

In the meantime, a pair of controversial calls during critical games aided replay's cause. For example, a key play in the Steelers' 1979 Super Bowl victory over the Cowboys was a pass interference call by field judge Fred Swearingen against Dallas cornerback Bennie Barnes on Lynn Swann. The 33-yard gain led to a Pittsburgh touchdown. However, replays showed Barnes tripped himself during incidental contact. The NFL regretted the officiating mistake and even wrote a letter of apology to a Cowboys fan. In 1980, the league admitted another mistake — a fumble by the Bears Walter Payton against the Falcons. Chicago lost the game and a playoff berth. The NFL later said Payton didn't fumble.

Replay arrives

Slowly, replay forces were gaining momentum. In 1985, the competition committee first approved use of instant replay for eight exhibition games, although the vote failed 16-8 (four didn't vote) for the 1985 regular season. During that preseason, 23 plays were reviewed, but only one was changed. This judicious use of the replay rule cleared the way for replay to enter the NFL on a full-time basis in 1986. The outcome of the historic vote of the owners at the March meeting at Rancho Mirage, Calif., was 23 in favor, four against and one abstention. The Cardinals, Giants, Chiefs and Broncos voted against it. The Steelers sat out because of a conflict of interest — Owner Art Rooney didn't want it, but coach Chuck Noll, who sat on the competition committee, did.

The landmark vote may have been prompted by controversy in another sport. The 1985 NFL season had its share of questionable flags and whistles. But the outcry for fairness in football was dwarfed by the din that descended upon baseball after the 1985 post-season. Don Denkinger's blown call in the sixth game of the 1985 World Series that kept alive the Kansas City Royals' game-winning rally was a deciding factor for some coaches.

"Suddenly, after that bad call, a lot of people realized they needed protection from the same thing," Cleveland Browns Owner Art Modell said. "(We) don't want a playoff game to be decided on a bad call."

The NFL approved a system intended to focus on plays of

possession — fumbles, interceptions and receptions — and most plays governed by the sideline. Replay would not be used to resolve penalties. The replay official in the press box would not be an NFL official, and conversations with the referee would be conducted via walkie-talkie.

No one was more pleased to see replay instituted than Cowboys President Tex Schramm, one of the earliest and most vociferous replay proponents. In many ways, instant replay was his baby — 10 years in the making and now, finally, a reality.

"This is probably one of the best decisions we've had at a league meeting in many years, as far as people expressing themselves and doing something to help the game," Schramm said. "Replay has become a fixture on television broadcasts, so we should use what the public sees."

Speaking for the dissenters, Chiefs coach John Mackovic said he didn't want to lose the game's human element. "I always enjoyed the shortcomings, knowing they were part of the game," he said.

During the meetings, it appeared at times the measure would fail. Owners weren't sure about the time frame. Should this be a permanent rule? Modell suggested adopting replay for one year. Like any new venture, this one would have bugs, he reasoned. Ironically, one of the first replay snafus went against Schramm's Cowboys in a preseason game when a beeper message to the umpire from the press box official, who wanted to overturn an error, failed.

The regular season opened and more problems unfolded, including:

• During a Monday night game, the Broncos lost a touchdown in a 21-10 victory over the Steelers. John Elway lateraled to running back Gerald Willhite, who threw a long touchdown pass to Steve Watson. Line judge Boyce Smith ruled Elway was guilty of a forward lateral, although the replay proved he wasn't. But the field officials didn't know the play was being reviewed and Denver ran another play, making it too late for the error to be corrected.

• The Dolphins griped when field officials didn't contact the press box to review a late fumble that cost them a game against the Jets.

• The Raiders scored a touchdown and shifted the momentum their way in an eventual victory over the Chiefs when quarterback Marc Wilson's TD pass to Dokie Williams was ruled a touchdown — but the replay official disagreed.

Jack Reader, the replay official, reviewed the 12-yard play and determined Williams landed only one foot in bounds before stepping out of bounds in the end zone. Reader used his walkie-talkie to announce his finding to umpire John Keck. Reader said, "Pass incomplete," but Keck heard, "Pass complete," so the touchdown stood.

Mackovic, an anti-replay coach, was understandably furious: "It's stinking lousy. We bring in people and we pay them. But when all is said and done, we can't even get them to communicate."

The following day, the NFL announced a "glossary of terms" to avoid such confusion in the future.

• The same day as the Chiefs-Raiders debacle, a replay official needed five minutes to untangle a call that ultimately wasn't overturned during a Cardinals-Giants game.

By midseason, talk began of chucking the whole deal. Replays were taking too long, because replay officials had to run through various angles and at times, watch a play repeatedly to reach a conclusion. Also, an inequity existed because the same number of cameras weren't available for all games. Teams pointed out that Monday night contests had a much better chance of clear-cut reviews because ABC used 12 cameras and the reverse angle. NBC and CBS worked with half that number of cameras on Sundays. Also, a group of owners complained that although instant replay was intended to remove human error, it was actually having the opposite effect. "It's not working," Bengals Owner Paul Brown said. "It has added a layer of error."

In response to these grievances, the NFL made changes. By mid-October, the walkie-talkie was replaced with a radio frequency. Umpires received messages from the press box through an earplug. Another policy switch: Replay officials were prohibited from discussing the system with reporters until after the season. In fact, one replay official backed out of a public speaking engagement when he heard reporters would be attending.

Living with gaffes

The number of goofs dwindled during the second half of the season, so the owners approved replay for 1987 by the slimmest of margins, 21-7 (it requires a 3/4 majority for passage). The effort would have failed without the intervention of Commissioner Pete Rozelle, who persuaded the competition committee to request a one-year reprieve rather than the two years they were seeking. Not even a mistake in the Super Bowl, when the Broncos lost a first-down completion (confirmed too late by replay) and Elway was sacked on the next play for the turning point of the Giants victory, halted the experiment.

The 1987 season passed without major incident, so the owners grew more confident. The next vote went 23-5 with the Steelers, Jets and Patriots switching sides. The Bills voted against the measure this time. Rooney, the Pittsburgh president, said he liked the modification introduced for the 1988 season: the replay officials would be part of the regular officiating crew, rather than staff members from the league office. Again, the competition committee sought two years but received just a one-year extension.

The vote went 24-4 for the 1989 season, but might have failed had it not been for Rozelle's retirement. Rozelle supported the use of replay, and most of the owners liked Rozelle. In a straw vote before Rozelle's announcement, 19 voted in favor. The Chiefs, long an opponent, switched their vote as a going-away gift. So did the Steelers, Bills and two others.

But 1989 proved to be a difficult year for replay. Against the

Saints, 49ers wide receiver Jerry Rice scored a touchdown, although the replay clearly showed he fumbled at the 1 yard line, and the ball squirted out of the back of the end zone. The 49ers kicked the extra point before the play could be reviewed, which meant the play couldn't be overturned. Later in the game, San Francisco receiver John Taylor scored the game-winning touchdown after it appeared he had been stripped of the ball.

The delays droned on. In a Steelers-Oilers game, five replay examinations stopped the game for a total of 14 minutes. On one occasion, 5 minutes and 32 seconds were required to pinpoint the spot of a completed pass. This hang-up was rectified for the 1990 season, when a two-minute time limit on replay review was imposed. The owners considered this modification, along with a report released by the league that delineated replay's imperfections, which included five incorrect reversals in 1989. Despite replay's flaws, the owners passed replay once again by a 21-7 margin.

But the owners' confidence began to erode in the new decade. Replay survived in 1990 when Eagles Owner Norman Braman cast the final vote. Ten months later, Philadelphia lost a touchdown in a playoff game against the Redskins when a review of the videotape wiped out Ben Smith's 87-yard fumble return. Two years later, the Eagles voted against replay.

Moreover, the NFL wasn't delivering on its promise to limit review time. During a Chiefs-Chargers game late in 1991, replay officials took eight minutes to review a play that ultimately wasn't changed. The owners decided they had seen enough inaction. Fans were griping loudly about delays. Replay was shown the door.

Good-bye, then hello, replay

The 1992 vote at the owners' meeting in Phoenix wasn't even close. Eleven teams — the Giants, Bengals, Cardinals, Chiefs, Bears, Bills, Lions, Cowboys, Jets, Eagles and Bucs — voted it down. The rule was in trouble from the first vote. Balloting proceeds in alphabetical order, but a different team starts the roll call each vote. The Cowboys, long a replay proponent, started the roll call for this vote and cast their ballot against replay.

"I think we'll have it back in a year," said Saints President Jim Finks, chairman of the competition committee.

The voice of reason belonged to the Raiders Al Davis. "We just need to learn how to use it better. We ought to develop it, but we have to go forward with the technology."

However, the NFL was in no hurry to continue developing instant replay. Even ongoing controversial calls couldn't swing enough votes. In 1996, the Packers Don Beebe scored on a 59-yard touchdown reception against the 49ers, but replays concluded he had been touched by a San Francisco defender while down. The Packers won in overtime and went on to win the Super Bowl. A 49ers victory would have given them home field advantage throughout the playoffs. Instead, they were a wild-card team.

A year later, replay proved another critical call with post-season implications was botched when Lions cornerback Bryant Westbrook was credited with a late-game end zone interception that ended a Jets drive. Replays revealed it shouldn't have counted. Detroit won and made the playoffs. The loss kept the

Jets, who had voted against replay the previous March, out of the post-season.

But once again, replay didn't make the cut after the 1997 season. Because the NFL added two expansion teams, 23 of 30 "yeas" were needed for replay to pass. Some were swayed; 21 voted for it.

Then came the 1998 season and with it, if not some of the worst officiating, certainly the worst case of officials-bashing in the history of the printed word. The few media types who cared to advance past the name-calling stage posited various theories for the deterioration of NFL zebra skills. For instance, the Steelers Rooney suggested the game had become too fast-paced — officials lived under incredible scrutiny by the league office and consequently, were so preoccupied with grading well that common sense was sacrificed. "They're so gun-shy now, they fear that if they make some little mistake, they're going to be graded down," Rooney said.

Former zebra Jim Tunney, one of the best in the game's history, pointed out that in the 1998 season, nearly 40 of 112 NFL officials had four years experience or less. He also stated it takes up to five years for an official from the college ranks to feel comfortable in the pros. Another former official, Ben Dreith, suggested the NFL was lax in training officials.

As always, the argument of converting officiating to a full-time occupation drew more than its share of support. However, that proposal has always been rejected by officials.

"We play only once a week," former Officials Supervisor Art

McNally said. "Proponents have said officials could be associated with particular teams and would be able to see things in practice. But pro teams don't scrimmage. An official would just be watching a series of drills under no pressure. If we also played at midweek, maybe one crew could do more than one game a week, but that's not going to happen."

One solution with nearly universal support was the return of instant replay, which easily passed. Only the Bengals, Cardinals and Jets voted against it. Coaches were satisfied with the latest revision: Two challenges were allowed during the initial 28 minutes of each half, with the team requesting the replay losing a timeout for each challenge not upheld. Challenges during the final two minutes of play were to be called from the press box by an NFL replay assistant with previous officiating experience. Transferring that decision from the coaches to the officials was a key element in the proposal. "That created a lot of sentiment for it," said Bucs coach Tony Dungy.

The 1999 exhibition season passed without major incident, but there were concerns. A challenge during a Titans-Chiefs game was unresolved because of technical difficulties. A digital computer system failed, so the replay crew had to use a backup video tape system. The review took about three minutes longer than the new 90-second time limit.

Other replay snafus included a call made during a Ravens victory over the Giants. New York's LeShon Johnson's fumble stood when it appeared he was down. Also, Baltimore's Billy Davis was credited with a 35-yard reception when his toe apparently touched the sideline. Replay didn't correct the mistakes.

But replay triumphed in a Bears-Steelers game. Pittsburgh appealed a safety that was called after a Steelers player tried to save a blocked punt from rolling out of the back of the end zone. The replay showed the player had control of the ball before going out of bounds for a touchdown.

In 63 preseason games, there were 47 coaches' challenges. Ten were upheld. In all, 14 on-field rulings were overturned. The average review time was 57 seconds, and the average delay was 2 minutes, 29 seconds. The NFL hoped to do better in the regular season.

Not for colleges

Instant replay for use in the college game is unlikely, because there are too many games, it's too expensive, and there are not enough qualified personnel. But the subject comes up occasionally, usually after a controversial call — for instance, during the Texas-Oklahoma game of 1984.

When Sooners defensive back Keith Stanberry was ruled not to have both feet down in the end zone, thereby nullifying an interception, the Longhorns were able to kick a field goal and forge a 15-15 tie. The game removed Oklahoma from the national championship picture and coach Barry Switzer threatened to blackball the official — prevent him from working future Sooners games — who made the call. But after cooling off, Switzer instead called for instant replay.

"Coaches and players put months of time, energy and effort into creating a good football team, and it comes down to one call, a judgement call, where the official wasn't in a position to make the decision. That's where we ought to use the visual aids and recorders, in championship games and games of significance," Switzer said.

Another significant game occurred early in the 1999 season. Michigan running back Anthony Thomas scored the winning touchdown against Notre Dame on a run from the 1. His knees were apparently down short of the goal line, before the ball made it across. The loss was more distasteful for Notre Dame because of a 15-yard excessive-celebration penalty against the Irish after Bobby Brown scored a two-point conversion. Brown put his thumbs in the ear holes of his helmet and waved his hands in a moose antler-like gesture. The penalty forced Notre Dame to kick off from its 20, and the Wolverines started their game-winning drive from their 42.

While a replay wouldn't have wiped out the penalty, it might have kept Michigan out of the end zone.

STRANGE CALLS

The lost down

December 8, 1968, the Los Angeles Rams lost a down and a chance at the playoffs.

The Bears led 17-16 with 35 seconds remaining. The Rams had reached the Chicago 32 and were closing in on field-goal range. On first down, Roman Gabriel threw an incomplete pass, and the Rams were called for holding. The Bears accepted the penalty and pushed Los Angeles back to its 47.

The down should have been repeated, but the sideline marker read, "second down." Gabriel tossed three straight incompletions. After the third, Chicago took over and ran out the clock. Sportswriters in the press box noticed the error, but no one on the field realized the mistake until it was too late.

Had the Rams won, their game the following week against the Colts would have been for the Western Division title. As it was, Baltimore clinched the title when Los Angeles lost.

Commissioner Pete Rozelle suspended referee Norm Schachter, a respected official, and his crew for the rest of the regular season and the post-season and issued this statement: "All six game officials are equally responsible for keeping track of downs. The crew which officiated the Los Angeles-Chicago game is considered among the best in pro football. However, because all six must bear responsibility for the error, the entire crew will receive no further assignments for the remainder of the 1968 NFL season and the entire post-season."

Immaculate demotion

Little did anyone know, when Franco Harris rolled into the end zone to complete the "immaculate reception" play that gave the Steelers a 13-7 AFC playoff victory over the Raiders in 1972, zebra Fred Swearingen was demoted.

"The game finished me as a referee," Swearingen told Bill Dwyre of *The Los Angeles Times*. "Shortly after that, I went back to being a field judge."

Swearingen admitted he never saw one of the most famous plays in football history, but that stands to reason. As the referee, his job was to keep his eyes on the quarterback.

"Until the end, it was a routine game. Oakland was leading 7-6 and Pittsburgh had a fourth-down play with about 40 seconds left. Terry Bradshaw went back to pass and Franco Harris swung out to the left. Now, as the referee, I'm with Bradshaw all the way. That's my job, to stay with him and look for roughing. I saw him throw the ball downfield, and by the time I looked up, Harris had the ball and was running down the sideline for a touchdown.

"There were fans on the field, and the security people were trying to clear them away. My officiating crew was scattered all over because a pass play forces them to do so. (Raiders coach) John Madden was screaming at me that whatever had just happened was illegal."

What had happened was Bradshaw's pass banged off intended receiver Frenchy Fuqua or Raiders defensive back Jack Tatum, or both. Everything would have been fine if it had caromed off

Tatum. But under the 1972 rules, the ball couldn't go from one offensive player to another.

"I got downfield as fast as I could, through fans, players, and even dogs, and gathered my crew. Then I polled them to find out what they saw. I ended up with four 'I don't knows,' including my own, and two 'I think the defensive man hit it.' Then I asked for sure if the defensive man hit it and nobody could say so."

There was speculation at the time that this was the first use of instant replay. After all, Swearingen walked over to a dugout and picked up a telephone. In the press box that day was Supervisor of Officials Art McNally. Seconds after hanging up, Swearingen signaled touchdown, but not because of an instant replay. McNally told him to clear the field and finish the game.

Fifth down, part I

November 16, 1940, powerhouse Cornell trailed Dartmouth 3-0 with a minute remaining when the Big Red drove to the 1. The Big Red was penalized five yards for delay of game. On fourth down, a pass in the end zone was batted down.

But as the Dartmouth players celebrated, referee Red Friesell, considered one of the game's top officials, signaled fourth down and placed the ball on the 6. Friesell had been confused by the scoreboard, which read, "third down" on the previous play. He was not overruled by any of the other three officials, and the Big Red made the most of their final chance: Quarterback Walt

Scholl lofted a touchdown pass to running back Bill Murphy.

"Just about everybody thought that was it," remembered Dartmouth coach Red Blaik, 30 years after the incident. "Everybody but our players, two of the officials and most of the writers up in the press box. They knew Cornell had scored on a fifth down. That's the way the sportswriters reported it."

Dartmouth students celebrated the outcome like a victory. Cornell Athletic Director Jim Lynah said if the officials told him there were five downs, he would surrender the victory. School President Dr. Ezra concurred. On Monday, Cornell officials studied the game film which proved the fifth down and telephoned Asa Bushnell, executive director of the Eastern Intercollegiate Association, to yield the victory.

If the schools needed more proof, after the game, Blaik drove Friesell to the train station. Along the way, Friesell admitted the mistake. Cornell coach Carl Snavely sent this telegram to Dartmouth:

"I accept the final conclusions of the officials and without reservation, concede the victory to Dartmouth with hearty congratulations to you and the gallant Dartmouth team."

In a most unusual twist, Friesell telegraphed an apology to Dartmouth captain Lou Young:

"I want to be the first to admit my very grave error on the extra down as proven by the motion picture of both colleges. I want to apologize to you, your players, coach Blaik and the assistant coaches ... I assume full responsibility. I want to thank you all for the very fair treatment accorded me after the game. Lou, I am so sorry, for you were such a grand captain and leader ..."

Fifth down, part II

October 6, 1990, Missouri led Colorado 31-27, but the Buffaloes had a first and goal at the Tigers 3. Here's the sequence of events:

First down, quarterback Charles Johnson deliberately spiked the ball to stop the clock. Second down, Eric Bieniemy rushed for two yards. Colorado took a timeout. It was at this point the down marker wasn't changed.

Third down, Bieniemy was stopped for no gain. The clock is stopped again with eight seconds left. Fourth down, Johnson spiked the ball again to stop the clock. He thought he could. After all, the down marker read "3."

Fifth down, Johnson scored on a keeper from the 1, even though it was questionable whether he crossed the goal line.

None of the officials immediately signaled TD, so Missouri fans started tearing down the goal post on the North end. But eventually, a line judge signaled a touchdown and Colorado had a 33-31 victory.

Missouri coach Bob Stull argued for 30 minutes after the game, but the outcome couldn't be reversed by rule. Unlike the Cornell-Dartmouth game of three decades earlier, Colorado wouldn't refuse the victory, although coach Bill McCartney felt public pressure to do so. Sadly, McCartney chose to blame Missouri's slippery artificial turf for the closeness of the game.

The crew was suspended for one game.

Referee J.C. Louderback retired after the season, tormented by the mistake.

"It boggles the mind," Louderback said. "All the players, all the coaches and all the officials — not one person noticed. It will always be an amazing thing in my mind. How could it have happened?"

The play was huge. Colorado, ranked 12th at the time, won the national championship that season. Ironically, the Buffaloes were helped by another official's call, when an apparent game-winning 91-yard punt return for a touchdown by Notre Dame's Rocket Ismail was nullified by a controversial clipping penalty in the Orange Bowl.

VOICES: Jim Tunney

Jim Tunney was an NFL official for 31 years and is widely regarded as one of the greatest. When he retired in 1991, Tunney had worked in a record 29 post-season games including three Super Bowls. He was on the field for such memorable moments as Bart Starr's quarterback sneak to win the 1967 NFL championship game known as the Ice Bowl, and Dwight Clark's back of the end zone catch to clinch the 49ers NFC championship victory over the Cowboys in 1982.

He is a motivational speaker and author of three books including his latest, *Chicken Soup for the Sports Fan's Soul.* Tunney talked about officiating, beginning with the timing of the 1998 season's controversial calls that led to the return of instant replay.

Put those situations in September and spread them out. Put one in the first week, one in the third and one in the fourth. Nothing would have been said. The impact would have been minimal. But because they were bunched up at the end of the season, involving teams fighting to reach the playoffs, it became a story. If you had included two teams that weren't going to make the playoffs, it would have been no big deal.

The biggest problem for officials is anticipation. It always has been, always will be. Veteran referees shouldn't anticipate, but they sometimes do. It can happen to anybody. (The Testaverde touchdown) was one of those cases. You know, a veteran player throws an interception, or makes some mistake. A coach makes a mistake or a bad call. It happens. I heard Joe Theismann say once when he was watching a tape of the Broncos, John Elway misread a coverage. Imagine, John Elway misreading a coverage. How could that happen? It's called human error. It's part of the game and it always will be, thank God. Actually, you can take it out of the game. It's called Madden 1999 *(a video game).*

Now, why do mistakes happen? I think one of the reasons the NFL has suffered is because there are quite a few new officials. In the early 1990s, our contracts increased considerably. We made a lot more money and officials hung on until age 60, 65, even 66. Now, you walk down the street of your hometown and pass a 66-year-old man and ask yourself if he could be an NFL referee.

I quit at 62. I thought I was a better referee at 62 than I was at 51, but I wasn't moving as well. That was apparent. Some officials hung on when they weren't moving as well. Then we lost eight, 10, 11 in a short time and they had to be replaced. Now, there's the factor of inexperience.

Last year, 35 to 40 of the 110 or so officials had four years or less of NFL experience. Now, almost 50 percent have five years or less. It takes somebody four or five years just to understand what it takes to be an NFL official, to understand NFL talent, just to get used to everything. It takes a long time to learn the philosophy.

Somebody once asked me why an official can't come into the league and have the impact that Randy Moss did as a player. Well, Randy Moss is an exception. Nothing I saw in Randy Moss in his first year made him look like a rookie.

We'll never go back to the good old days, but I started in 1960 as a field judge and worked with some great officials — some of the greatest ever. We didn't have crews in those days, so I had a plethora of officiating models. Those guys actually trained the younger officials. Nowadays, training comes from the office. Once the season starts, I'd like to see training turned over to the referee. I'd like to see the referee tell the field judge he needs to move a yard back, not have the philosophy come from the central office.

Officials are afraid of getting downgraded; they're so afraid of grades today. I wish they would throw those damn things out and just officiate the game. It doesn't seem to be as much fun as it was a few years ago. It ought to be fun. Grades are used only to beat up an official. You can't beat a guy up like that and expect him to work at a higher level. Those grades just tear a guy down.

I was working an exhibition game in 1978, and Art McNally was there, but he wouldn't tell my why. Afterward, he told me he was up in the booth looking at instant replay as a possible tool. Seven years later, I got a call from Art, who was in Maui for the NFL meetings. The competition committee was there. He asked me what I thought about instant replay. I asked him if I had a vote. He said I didn't, so I said, "What are you asking me for?"

My feeling was — I and my crew work the game. You want to change the rules, you want a 120-yard field? Fine. Want to change the shape of the ball? Fine. Just let us know what the rules are. I told Art, I thought some officials would be intimidated, but it wasn't going to affect my crew on the field.

In my public speaking, I talk about zero defect. If Chrysler puts out 1,000 cars and 999 are perfect but one's a lemon, that guy with the lemon's going to think Chrysler is a terrible company run by a bunch of bums. That's how it is in officiating. You make 1,000 calls, get all but one right, but because of the one you miss, everybody calls you a bum.

I said to my crew, "Let's see if we can go to zero defects and not even think about the guy in the booth during the game." But the IRO (instant replay official) was part of our crew. He attended rules meetings and went to pregame meals with us. I wanted that official to understand the guys on the field and where they positioned themselves.

That first year, our crew had one replay reversal all season. The next, same thing, one reversal. I thought the replay raised our level of intensity. It made us even sharper because we didn't want to be reversed. You know, the IRO had to be just as sharp. He didn't want to get it wrong and hear about it the next Tuesday from the NFL. The name of this job is focus. Lose it for a split second and it makes a big difference. We emphasized how important it was not to lose focus when plays were being checked by replay.

I saw Don Shula recently. He asked me what I thought about replay coming back. He remembered a game with something like 23 stoppages. Originally, the owners talked about using it just to review the big stuff. Then two or three years into it, the owners said they were putting a lot of money into it and wanted to make more effective use of it. I remember a game where there were 13 stoppages in the first quarter. It was terrible.

Look, it can be a good system when the NFL sticks to the basics like goal line calls, sideline plays and the end zone. I saw a preseason game (Steelers-Bears) where a punt was blocked, the ball rolled to the back of the end zone, the player recovered and the original call was a safety. The call was challenged, the replay showed the player who recovered had possession before he went out of the end zone, so the play was ruled a touchdown. That's the ideal scenario for using instant replay.

Then I saw another game (Cowboys-Browns) where a forward progress call at midfield was challenged. I thought, "That's where you don't need the replay." Let the officials call the play.

VOICES: Jerry Markbreit

Jerry Markbreit was one of the NFL's best officials before retiring after the 1998 season at the age of 64. He worked his way up the ladder from high schools to the Big Ten, then joined the NFL staff in 1976. He worked for the 3M Company in Chicago for 38 years. In 1988, he wrote his autobiography, *Born to Referee*.

Officiating is a very noble profession, performed by people of the highest integrity. They take constant criticism, they understand abuse goes with the territory, but most spend their adult lives trying to improve and perfect their skills.

You know it's a tough profession. The first football game in America was between Princeton and Rutgers in 1869. After the game, one of the school newspapers said the officiating was the worst they'd ever seen. This was after the first game!

I began officiating at age 21 and retired at 64. I've worked all there is to work — the Rose Bowl, eight NFC and AFC championship games, four Super Bowls and 25 playoff games. I've seen it all. (Regarding the 1998 season), those same mistakes happen every year. Unfortunately, they don't always happen at a high profile time or as closely as the ones (in 1998) did. Mistakes are made. I made them. Every official has made a mistake.

The officials in the NFL are the best in the country. Nobody becomes an NFL official haphazardly. They're taken from the top college conferences. They're interviewed, screened, scrutinized. They've been scouted and they are the very best. Candidates go through an extensive program just to get on the short list. Training methods are better than ever. Today, there's much greater demand placed on officials than in the old days.

Most don't come into the NFL until they're in their 40s, with 20 years of officiating on other levels. I was a rookie at 41, but I had been officiating for 20 years.

The technological advances have been remarkable. The technology is so good nowadays that you can take one second of action and turn it into about 30 individual frames of video. The 29th frame could show the ball coming out of a receiver's hands a quarter-inch from the ground. That's what appears on television. After they've gotten two or three looks at it, the reaction is, "My God, they've blown the call." But officials live with it. We always have.

Replay shouldn't matter to officials, and as far as I'm concerned, it doesn't. Instincts picked up from years of training tell you how to call them. You can't worry about replay. Umpires who make calls at first base can't be worried about the replay. Neither can a football official.

If you're worried about it, you can't officiate. If you're thinking about what a replay might show, your head's not in the right place. If you're thinking about anything except the game, you're in trouble.

You know, officials work full-time. They just have other jobs. Officials must have a job that allows them to take time off when the league asks. When an official comes into the NFL, he comes in as a mature person, somebody who has experience in the business world, with raising a family and dealing with people. That's important.

I figured I spent at least 40 hours a week on football before I left for a game. My final five years, I was retired from my job. Essentially, I was a full-time official. Those final five years I probably spent about 60 hours a week on football before I left for a game.

Sportswriters must hate us. Pro football is the only sport that hasn't elected officials to its Hall of Fame. Names of officials have been on the ballots. Nobody's in. That's a shame.

Chapter 3

HOCKEY/BASKETBALL

THE PUCK STOPS HERE
AND THE NBA OFFICIALLY SPEAKS

Let's go to the video ...

Until the final goal, the 1999 Stanley Cup Finals had been a mixture of outstanding goaltending by Ed Belfour of the Dallas Stars and Dominik Hasek of the Buffalo Sabres, clutch goal scoring by the Stars Joe Nieuwendyk, and general disbelief among the spectators that the Cup might end up in Texas.

But with 14 minutes and 51 seconds expired in the third overtime, all of this was forgotten as the Stanley Cup plunged into its most controversial moment in more than a century of playoff action. Never had a final hockey series — perhaps any major championship game — ended with such a questionable call.

There was no doubt the Stars Brett Hull had his left skate in the crease when he knocked the puck past Hasek on a rebound, giving Dallas the 2-1 victory and the series triumph in six games. A skate in the crease is considered goalie interference — a rule violation. A skate can only be in the crease if the attacking player is ahead of the puck and controls the puck. Such goals had been routinely nullified since the league cracked down on crease encroachment by video replay three years earlier. Video review had been part of the NHL since the 1991-92 season at the request of officials.

When Hull scored, there was no immediate problem. An exhausted Hasek lay prone on the ice and did not protest. Nor did his teammates, who lined up and prepared for the traditional series-ending handshake as the Stars celebrated their first Stanley Cup championship in franchise history.

No one in the press box questioned the goal or called attention to a possible violation. However, Sabres coach Lindy Ruff saw a replay of the goal in his office 20 minutes later on ESPN, which had broadcast the game and whose announcers were questioning the goal. ESPN analyst Barry Melrose, a former coach, said the goal shouldn't have been allowed.

Announcer Gary Thorne said, "This is really terrible. The Cup has been skated around the ice. This is the worst way the NHL could have ended this game. I don't mean to detract (from the Stars victory), but the NHL has to answer for this."

In a bizarre scene, Ruff rushed back to the ice and demanded a response as NHL Commissioner Gary Bettman was presiding over the Stanley Cup presentation. Ruff's main contention: "I wanted Bettman to answer as to why there was no review." Ruff later told reporters, "He almost turned his back on me. There was no answer. There was no review. It was as if he knew it was tainted."

The Sabres charged that once the Stars celebration began, the goal wouldn't be overturned. "Pandemonium sets in, so they don't go back and review it," Ruff said.

Hasek echoed his coach.

"I don't know what the video judge was doing," he said. "Maybe he was in the bathroom. Or maybe he was sleeping. Or maybe he doesn't know the rule. Or maybe the video was broken."

None of that was true. There had been a review. Bryan Lewis, the league's director of officiating, insisted he and replay official Scott Brinkman reviewed the tape a dozen times while the Stars were celebrating. They ruled the goal legal. Lewis said Hull had possession throughout the sequence, but the referees did not seek a review from the video judge.

It was Lewis who met with the media in the wee hours to explain the non-call and to announce all NHL teams recently had been warned about such circumstances.

"March 25, we sent a memo to all the managers, listing the criteria for allowing goals to stand with a player in the crease, and the goal in question falls into one of those areas," Lewis said. "Hull played the puck. He had possession. A save (by Hasek) was made, which does not indicate change of possession. The rebound came off the goalie, which does not change anything. Hull had continuous possession, which makes it a good goal."

The memo, sent by NHL Senior Vice-President Colin Campbell to general managers and other team officials, addressed various issues, and crease encroachment specifically in Section 9.

"An attacking player maintains control of the puck, but skates into the crease before the puck enters the crease and shoots the puck into the net. Result: Goal is allowed."

But sportswriters covering the Cup, many of whom had seen nearly every regular-season NHL game, claimed they had never seen a crease violation overturned on that basis. The type of goal Hull scored had been consistently waved off during the regular season and playoffs.

Also, according to the rules, replay officials are responsible for notifying the on-ice officials if a player was in the crease at the time of a goal. The officials then confer to determine if the circumstances made a replay unnecessary. Officials Bill McCreary and Terry Gregory were not part of the decision-making process.

Lewis insisted that if the goal had been illegal, a horn would have sounded, the celebration would have ceased and play would have continued.

The following day, Commissioner Bettman stood by his officials in his public comment. "The rule was absolutely, correctly applied," Bettman said. "It was a non-issue. Everyone understands it was the right call."

Not in Buffalo. Ruff remained unconvinced the NHL acted properly. Addressing a crowd of 20,000 gathered to celebrate the Sabres outstanding season in front of City Hall, Ruff said he wanted to leave the fans with two words: "No goal." That set off a chant of, "No goal, no goal" from the fans. Some carried signs reading, "We were cheated, not defeated" and "Thou shalt not steal." The rally had started with fans chanting, "One more game, one more game."

Then, in a lovely piece of irony, NHL officials met one day after the controversial finish. During that meeting, they voted to eliminate the use of video replays to determine crease violations on goals, thereby shifting the responsibility to the on-ice officials. The meeting of the league's board of governors had already been scheduled, and the replay vote was on the agenda. But, in light of recent events, any dissension had no chance of being heard.

"To rely on replay too much isn't good," Bettman said. "The fact that so many people didn't understand the rule and how it was applied in that situation — and that you had controversy on a correct call — simply cemented the fact that there was a better way to do it. We're leaving the crease to a judgement call. This way is better for the game and better for the fans."

Too many good goals were being nullified by technicalities, and it was detrimental to the sport to wait two minutes to decide whether a goal was good, Bettman correctly stated. As the rule was written, Hull's goal was good. As the rule was practiced, the Sabres and Stars should have continued into the morning.

"It's a stupid rule, anyway," Hull said. "A stupid, stupid rule. Goalies can go all over the place, but when they're in the net, they can't go into the crease. Either keep them there or don't worry about this. If my toe is in the crease, I'm not interfering with anybody."

The NHL agreed; that's why the Stars paraded around the Stanley Cup that night. That's also why Sabres fans will forever believe they were cheated out of a chance to continue the game.

Controversy surrounding the officials isn't new to the Stanley Cup. Also, relations between referees and coaches reached an all-time low during the 1988 semifinals, moments after the Boston Bruins 6-1 victory over the New Jersey Devils in the third game. Devils coach Jim Schoenfeld waited for referee Don Koharski to leave the ice, then approached him on the runway leading to the dressing rooms.

"You're crazy, you're crazy," yelled Schoenfeld. "You fat pig. Go have another doughnut."

Koharski claimed Schoenfeld pushed him — a charge Schoenfeld denied.

The "doughnut" comment became a laughing matter, but the NHL was not amused. Even without a hearing, the league suspended Schoenfeld for the fourth game. However, Devils General Manager Lou Lamoriello, angered that his coach didn't receive a hearing, got a temporary restraining order from Superior Court Judge James F. Madden, barring the suspension. The court order was announced just 25 minutes before the start of the game.

But when the teams took the ice, there were no officials. Two minutes before the game was to begin, NHL Director of Officiating John McCauley approached the Devils bench. He told Schoenfeld the crew of referee Dave Newell, linesmen Ron Asselsine and Ray Scapinello with backup referee Denis Morel, refused to work if Schoenfeld stayed behind the bench. "I guess we won't have a game," Schoenfeld replied.

There was a game, but it was played only after the league scraped up amateur officials. Referee Paul McInnis and linesmen Vincent Goldeski and Jim Sullivan took the ice an hour after game time. The game actually commenced after a 67-minute delay. The linesmen wore green Devils sweat pants and yellow Bruins practice jerseys in the first period while official uniforms were being located.

Several fights broke out in the second period, including two brawls that led to 12 penalties. In all, 17 penalties were called in the second period. McCauley sat in one of the penalty boxes during the game to assist the officials. Before the start of the game, McCauley read a statement that appeared to support the officials, although the league was required to remain neutral publicly:

"NHL game officials scheduled to work tonight's contest made a personal decision that they could not perform their duties given the circumstances of Devils coach Jim Schoenfeld assuming a position behind the New Jersey bench. The officials were informed of their contractual obligations to work tonight's game, but they maintain their position."

New Jersey won the game 3-1, to even the series at 2-2. No sanctions were made against the boycotting officials — further evidence the NHL quietly supported their decision.

Boring basketball

Avery Johnson's baseline jumper made NBA champions of the San Antonio Spurs in 1999. It also ended a season which held the dubious distinction of producing less action than any previous year in league history.

The season had already been reduced to 50 games because of the lockout. On top of that, scoring dipped to an all-time low 91.6 points since the inception of the shot clock in 1954.

One cause of the lack of production is the game's physical nature. Basketball experts agree this shift in manner of play began with the defensive style of the Detroit Pistons, who won NBA championships in 1989 and 1990. Since then, the NBA has been reduced to a plodding, grinding, poor-shooting, game of intimidation that was masked by the excellence of Michael Jordan.

How important is the game's style? Consider this: television ratings for the regular season and playoffs were down considerably in 1999. Fans tuned into an NBA game expecting to see the graceful forms of the world's greatest athletes. Instead, they watched brutes who patrol the lanes like armored guards, forcing the watchable action away from the basket.

In Jordan's first year of permanent retirement, NBA officials addressed the issue of scoring with a 16-member special rules committee of players, coaches and front office personnel.

The committee met during the NBA Finals and made several suggestions that were adopted. Defensive players now can't make contact with hands or forearms outside of the free-throw line extended. A player has to shoot, pass or pick up his dribble within five seconds if he begins dribbling with his back to the basket (the Charles Barkley rule). And the shot clock is reset to 14 seconds for several violations. Teams used to get a fresh 24. After one month of the regular season, teams averaged five more field-goal attempts per game.

What would the official's role be in all this? NBA Deputy Commissioner Russ Granik and league Senior Vice-President Rod Thorn answered that question and others during the NBA Finals. Some excerpts include:

Q: What was the prevailing sentiment about what officials should do about (excessive) contact?

Granik: Clearly, the sentiment was we must have less contact. This is not intended as a knock on the officials; they're calling the game as best they can, the way they've been trained to call it. But the game has evolved to a point where there is just too much contact, particularly away from the ball. The hope is if we come up with the right combination of strategies that allow more movement away from the ball, teams won't have the same incentive on every play to throw it into the post.

Q: How is this going to affect scoring?

Granik: Scoring is not the only issue. If we come out of this with a game that looks better but the scores are about the same as they are now, I don't think anyone on our committee would think that's a failure. It wasn't a mandate just to increase scoring. We certainly would like to end the decrease we've seen over the last decade. Simply increasing scoring wasn't our particular goal. You can do that by making the basket larger or playing 15-minute quarters.

Q: About 10 years ago when the third referee was added, the explanation was he was going to call fouls away from the ball. Why hasn't that worked?

Granik: It's not about what the referees see or don't see. It's more about how they've become accustomed to calling and what people have come to accept as appropriate. Why it's evolved to the point where certain types of contact that might have been called 20 years ago aren't called today, I don't know. That's a philosophical question none of us can answer.

Q: Your critics will say you're making up rules to hide deficiencies of players. Do you buy into that?

Granik: If anything, the (committee's) view was that players have become better, particularly on defense. They're bigger, faster and stronger than in the past. They're better coached, started their basketball lives earlier and have been playing defense straight through. That's why we have to keep the rules up with whatever is happening on the court and how the players are (developing).

Q: You don't have any referees on the committee.

Granik: I think in the NBA, the referees will officiate the way they're instructed, to the best of their abilities.

Q: Ed Rush's input — did he have any suggestions on how to clarify the rules to make the job of referees easier?

Granik: Ed is particularly helpful in telling the committee and us what is easier for a referee to do on the floor. During consideration of the five-second rule, his role was very important because there was discussion of other ways you might be able to limit or eliminate the back down in the post.

STRANGE CALLS

A matter of timing

Alabama's second-round victory over UCLA in the 1998 Midwest Regional cost three officials advancement in the NCAA women's tournament.

The problem started when, with 1.8 seconds remaining, the Bruins Maylana Martin hit a free throw for a 74-73 lead. She missed the second, and Alabama got a time-out with 0.8 seconds remaining.

The officials then made the first of three mistakes. Referee Jack Riordan told Alabama guard Brittney Ezell she could run the baseline on the inbounds pass. This was a mistake. Players can run the baseline only after a made basket or free throw.

Ezell ran the baseline and threw a three-quarter length pass that was tipped by UCLA's Erica Gomez and Alabama's Dominique

Canty. (That's when the clock should have started.) Canty's deflection went to teammate LaToy Caudle, who banked in a jumper from the top of the key for the winning points.

In all, it took nearly three seconds for the sequence to play out, but the clock never started until Caudle got the ball. UCLA coach Pam Oliver immediately protested, but the officials then made their third mistake by running off the floor without first checking the television replay monitors, which is allowed to settle clock disputes. A correctable error, the NCAA calls it.

For 90 minutes, UCLA players remained on the floor, hopeful of a reversal. But it couldn't happen. Once the officials leave the court, the result stands. The NCAA suspended the crew for the rest of the tournament and issued an apology.

"The ending of the game was an unfortunate and regrettable situation. It is unfortunate when the outcome of a game is influenced by factors other than the participants on the floor."

An American nightmare

A communications breakdown and questionable interpretation of the rules contributed to the controversial — and painful for Americans — finish to the 1972 Olympic gold medal basketball game.

The stage: The United States had never lost an Olympic basketball game (62-0) heading into the finals in Munich. But the Soviet Union had played well and seemed poised to pull off the upset, leading by eight with 6 minutes and 7 seconds to play. Then, coach Hank Iba's team turned on the defense with a full-court press and closed to 44-42.

Russia held a 49-48 lead and the ball, when Doug Collins picked up a loose ball at midcourt with six seconds left and was hammered going in for a layup at three seconds.

Collins, the cool Illinois State guard who went on to an NBA playing and coaching career, sank both free throws. Just before he shot the second free throw, the horn sounded because Soviet coach Vladimir Kondrashkin wanted a timeout. But the ball was already in Collins' hands, and under the rules, the timeout could not be called.

After Collins swished the second shot, the Soviets took the ball out under their basket. The pass was deflected as two seconds ran off the clock. Fans rushed the court. The game was stopped to clear the floor. The final second was played and the horn sounded as the Americans started celebrating.

But Kondrashkin and the Soviet coaches were arguing they again had demanded a timeout. At this point, Robert William Jones, secretary-general of the game's international ruling body (FIBA), made his way from the stands to the scorer's table and listened to Kondrashkin's protests. Jones, who had no authority to do so under the rules, awarded the Soviets a timeout and ordered three seconds back on the clock.

On this inbounds pass, Modestas Paulauskas missed a desperation shot and the horn sounded. Again, the Americans celebrated. Again, the Russians protested, claiming the ball had been put in play before the clock had been properly reset. Jones gave the Soviets three more seconds.

This time it paid off. A desperation pass traveled the length of the floor to Russia's best player, the husky 6-8 Aleksander Belov, who was guarded by Americans Kevin Joyce and James Forbes. The three players went up, both Americans went down. Belov came down with the ball, went back up and dropped in a layup, touching off a Soviet celebration.

The Bulgarian referee signed the score sheet. Renato Righetto, an official from Brazil, refused to sign in protest. It was his fourth Olympic final, and he knew an injustice had occurred. Iba also refused to sign and protested the outcome. A five-member jury considered the argument and upheld the Russian victory in a 3-2 vote. The three votes for the Soviets came from Communist-bloc nations.

The bitter American team didn't show up to collect the first silver medal in its Olympic hoop history.

VOICES: Scott Thornley

One of college basketball's top officials, Thornley has worked two NCAA title games, including the 1999 final between Connecticut and Duke. He is a retired teacher who lives in Pocatello, Idaho. He offered his thoughts on basketball officiating.

I don't think you can generalize and say today's game is more intense for officials. Arenas vary. Crowds vary. Some basketball venues are more sophisticated than others, and in these places, the crowds react to officiating differently. These fans appreciate the nature of the game; they appreciate good basketball. Then you go into other arenas, where a university hasn't had much success, and that frustration can spill over to the officiating. We become the ones they blame. It's not easy for those fans to accept that their team may have missed eight or 10 free throws. We're probably not as good as we think we are, but not as bad as the fans think we are.

We officials have much more exposure than before. It used to be a big deal to call a game that was on TV. But with ESPN, Fox and all the others, whether you call a game in the West, East, South or Midwest, people in that arena know who you are.

One difference over the years is that officiating isn't as regionalized as it once was. In the past, you could tell what part of the country you were in by the way the game was called. Therefore, when teams went on the road, they wanted officials from their conference to call the game. Nowadays, there's a national coordinator of officials. We mix and match from coast to coast, and if you didn't call the game the same way everywhere, you'd stick out like a sore thumb. As far as the officials are concerned, we've become much more similar over the years.

I started in 1978 when I was 21. I began officiating with the Big Sky Conference, which was unique because we drove to every game. Sometimes that meant a drive of six to eight hours. We'd get $75 a game and $40 per diem. The easiest part of those days was the game.

As for instant replay, I don't feel threatened by it. Most of the time, if a there's a replay, the call could go either way. Generally speaking, I'm satisfied when I watch games and see the replays. It shows pretty much the same thing I saw. But you're always going to have calls that are wrong. In this business, everybody wants you to be perfect — then get better.

We work a lot of games. You don't hear about pro officials being overworked, though. No college official I know that works a lot doesn't take care of himself. The job is too important to them. You don't hear about NBA officials who worked in Los Angeles one night and Chicago the next being overworked. In college, sometimes that's an excuse. Coaches will search for any excuse to blame the officials. It's like the old comment, "Let the kids decide the game." We do. But we also get paid to referee the game from the top to the final buzzer. If somebody commits a foul and a call has to be made, we make it. Everything revolves around contact, and if it affects normal play, it's a foul at 15:30 or with 30 seconds to play.

Make up calls? I've never heard officials talk about them. You have to be pretty much focused on the action. Now, you might have calls that are similar. That just happens, but fans may not think so.

We know we're not going to make everybody happy. If we can be satisfied with ourselves, and make our supervisors happy, that's good. College basketball is a great game and a tough game. Coaches' jobs and reputations are on the line because of two factors: how 18 and 19-year-old players will react under pressure, and how 40 and 50-year-old coaches will react under pressure. As officials, it's better to be treated with respect and to be trusted than it is to be liked.

The Connecticut-Duke game was great — very well played. As officials, we couldn't have asked for a better game. There were no big problems, just great action. The NCAA tournament is big time pressure, and every step you take in the tournament, the pressure becomes greater. You've got to have a pretty strong constitution to stay focused and not get caught up in the spotlight and the glare.

Chapter 4

BOXING/OTHER SPORTS

SITTING IN JUDGMENT

"I'm sorry, I made a mistake"

How long is the list of boxing's most disgraceful moments? The deaths in the ring, the ears chewed off, the dives, kickbacks, bribes and scandals. It takes a mighty wallop to give boxing a black eye, but that's just what happened March 13, 1999, in New York before 21,000 at Madison Square Garden and millions of witnesses who shelled out $49.95 on pay-per-view.

When the 12-round heavyweight fight was over, Lennox Lewis lifted his arms in triumph, and Evander Holyfield, a proud but beaten warrior, slumped in his corner, his face bloodied. His prediction of a third-round knockout seemed ridiculous. Lewis had pummeled Holyfield throughout the fight and had clearly won.

Except two of the three fight judges saw it differently. The card of Eugenia Williams of New Jersey, representing the International Boxing Federation, showed Holyfield winning,

115-113. The 115-115 score on the card of Britain's Larry O'Connell seemed very generous to Holyfield. South African judge Stanley Christodoulou favored Lewis 116-113.

Round winners get 10 points, losers nine points. If the round is scored a draw, each gets 10 points. Each judge scored Lewis as winning the first two rounds and Holyfied the third. After that, the Christodoulou card favored Holyfield only three more times. O'Connell had Holyfield winning four more rounds and Williams' card gave Holyfield six of the final nine rounds.

Lewis actually had to win the final round in order to survive the draw. O'Connell awarded Lewis round 12 to even his card.

If the scores were tabulated by simply adding the points or the rounds, Lewis would have won by a razor-thin margin, but that's not how it works. One judge had Lewis winning, another gave it to Holyfield and a third called it dead even. It adds up to a draw that left the Lewis camp outraged, and promoter Don King licking his chops at the notion of a rematch. "Don't be afraid," King told the press after the fight. "If you think Holyfield lost the fight, go ahead and say so."

That's not all they said. The judging was deemed such a travesty in the boxing world, three separate New York authorities investigated the bout armed with the numbers that supported a Lewis victory. He landed 348 of 613 punches for a connection rate of 57 percent. Holyfield connected on 130 of 385 punches, or 34 percent. Although the judges' cards were split, every media service covering and scoring the event had Lewis winning easily.

The investigation centered around Williams and King, who

needed a Holyfield victory or a draw to control the rematch and the glamorous heavyweight division. Had Lewis won, King would have lost his top money producer in Holyfield. Also, Williams represented the IBF. That organization recognizes Holyfield as the world champion. Lewis is the World Boxing Council champion. A unified champion was to emerge.

"Judging in an athletic contest is always a subjective process," said New York State Attorney General Eliot Spitzer. "In this case, however, the judges' decision was out of line with the reality of the situation and has raised legitimate questions of tampering, incompetence or both."

King's response: "My job is to present a great event and to sell tickets, not to select judges or determine the outcome of the fight in any way. Anytime you have human judgment involved in making calls, you may have a certain amount of conflict. These decisions involve people making subjective calls and judgments. Those decisions can be extremely controversial.

"Perception is reality. If you look at the perception, I'm to blame for the Johnstown flood, World War II and the San Francisco fire. Anything they can find, they blame on me."

Investigators wanted to know if Williams was bribed. Was she in King's pocket? Williams had entered the fight with an impressive resumé: More than 90 fights, including 27 title bouts to her credit. But her credentials were questionable. When Lewis landed a flurry of blows in a dominating fifth round, Williams said her view was obscured because Lewis' back was to her. (Lewis was criticized by boxing experts for not being more aggressive in the fifth when he had Holyfield on the ropes. A knockout punch would have avoided the controversy.)

"I couldn't see the blows I later saw on TV," Williams told investigators. "I'm taking a lot of heat, but I can't score what I can't see. I scored what I saw. As long as you're honest, people can say what they want to say."

Williams added that after reviewing the fight film, she would have changed her score, giving the fifth round to Lewis, who landed 43 punches to Holyfield's 11. But that wouldn't have altered the outcome.

More questions were raised after revelations that Williams had filed for Chapter 7 bankruptcy. She had more than $33,000 in credit card debt. Williams, who works as a $39,200-a-year accounts clerk for the city of Atlantic City, N.J., listed assets of $56,889, and liabilities of $72,109, in her filing seven weeks before the fight.

Unflattering news leaked like a sieve. Williams had been fired from the World Boxing Union a year earlier for not being a team player.

But she had her supporters. IBF President Bob Lee, whose organization selected Williams, defended her work. "I am sure they aren't going to find anything irregular," he said. "It is a subjective viewing of a fight, and you can't tell these judges what to see or what not to see. All I tell them is, 'Do the best you can.'

"She has impeccable credentials. She attends seminars and takes an active part in them. She is a professional. When I appointed her, I expected her to record what she saw. If she says that's what she saw, then I support her."

Williams is a lifelong boxing fan. In her teens, she trained as a boxer, but turned to karate when she found no opportunities for female boxers. She began judging amateur fights in 1983, moving to the pro ranks in 1989. Williams was paid $1,600 for this fight.

Another investigation was launched in Nevada when gaming officials reported a flood of late money, more than $1 million, was bet on Holyfield just before he stepped into the ring. Almost all of the money ended up being refunded because of the draw. A longtime Las Vegas bettor said the late money was so unusual, he suspected the bets were made with inside knowledge of the outcome.

Within a week, the fighters agreed to a rematch. Their reactions to the squabble were predictable.

Lewis: "I won the fight. It was my time to shine and they ripped me off. I'm the undisputed heavyweight champion of the world, and the whole world knows it. (Holyfield) should give me the belts because he knows they're mine. If Evander's a man, he should admit he got beat and give me the belts. You could say he's holding them for me now. They're mine. He knows it, and he's just holding them for me.

"In this particular fight, the public got hurt as well as the fighter. I say Don King and the judges should apologize. Next time I'm going to bring my two judges, my own two judges.

"In the fifth, Evander wasn't hurt as badly as I thought. I wasn't satisfied I could feel safe. He was definitely playing possum. But if I had known it was going to be scored like that, I would have realized my only hope was a knockout, and I would have gone after it."

Holyfield: "The judges said it was a draw. Realistically, he didn't knock me out, and I didn't knock him out. Even with the punch stats, people say, 'Well, this man hit you 600 times.' But if he hit me that much, why didn't I fall? How come I never staggered or was hurt? Obviously, a lot of times he was tapping me.

"I was trying to get him close to me so I could nail him with a big shot. But it didn't work. When boxers don't do what they're supposed to do, it falls into the judges' hands.

"I was cramping. I couldn't shift my weight properly. From the first round, I started catching cramps in my legs. The only time I could hit him was when he got close enough. When I pushed off, I was getting cramps in my legs.

"It's real simple. (Fans) are not the judges. That's the way it goes. I feel like the heavyweight champion of the world."

The New York investigations produced new regulations involving judges. Under the new rules, judges must be sanctioned by the state. Also, judges who live in or are licensed in other states or nations must submit a sworn application for a license. Judges would be subject to a credit check, which would disclose pending litigation such as bankruptcy; the check would also reveal financial ties to a boxer, promoter or television company.

In addition, each sanctioning body with an interest in the title fight must submit a list of three judge candidates, not just one candidate, with the state boxing commission to select the judge after a background check. The commission has the power to reject any nomination, as it sees fit.

Finally, what of O'Connell, the British judge who scored the fight a draw? Had he given Lewis, his fellow countryman, one more round, there would have been no outcry, no controversy, no investigation. From rounds 6-12, O'Connell favored Holyfield 4-1-2. Williams had Lewis winning three of those rounds.

O'Connell was just as much to blame for the outcome as Williams, and he also was part of the investigation. But we didn't find out about his bank records or see his life story splashed across newspapers. Unlike Williams, O'Connell admitted he erred.

"I'm sorry, I made a mistake," O'Connell told *The Sun*, a London tabloid. "I honestly thought Lewis had nicked it (won). I thought he'd won it with his left jab alone. When someone said my scorecard added up to a draw, my heart sank. I was as surprised as anyone. Judged on the weight of opinion, I would say I was wrong. But I did what I thought was right at the time. I can't be more honest than that."

Holyfield-Lewis scorecards

Round	O'Connell		Christodoulou		Williams	
	H	**L**	**H**	**L**	**H**	**L**
1	9	10	9	10	9	10
2	9	10	9	10	9	10
3	10	9	10	9	10	9
4	9	10	9	10	10	9
5	9	10	9	10	10	9
6	10	9	9	10	9	10
7	10	10	9	10	9	10
8	10	9	10	9	10	9
9	10	9	10	9	10	9
10	10	10	10	9	10	9
11	10	9	10	10	10	9
12	9	10	9	10	9	10
totals	115	115	113	116	115	113

VOICES: Mills Lane

He's a courtroom judge and veteran boxing referee, who was in the ring the night Mike Tyson bit off a chunk of Evander Holyfield's ear. In light of a boxing death (the recent passing of Randie Carver in Kansas City), I asked Lane about a referee's role.

It's one of the reasons a referee shouldn't score the fight. In the old days, the referee did. But your focus is entirely different than a judge's. Your job is to see if the fight is being fought closely. If it's close, the referee shouldn't even know who's ahead.

A rule I always tried to follow is, once a fight is no longer competitive, when one man is getting shellacked, then the fight should be stopped.

If a kid takes a straight shot and you see the head begin to roll around, then he's in real trouble. If a fighter is in that position, I don't believe he should take another punch, even if the ref has to take a punch himself.

I look for general fatigue — whether a fighter is able to defend himself. I look at the legs. Are the legs doing something other than what the brain is telling them to do? I also look at the eyes. I don't care what a fighter is telling me. I want to know what the eyes are telling me. How does he look? Is he focusing on me?

Finally, it's a sense thing. I don't think it's absolutely imperative that a referee be a former fighter. But it can help. Every fighter's gotten his bell rung. When you're in the ring as a ref and you see a kid getting his bell rung, you know what he's going through. You've been there. That means you've got to be in shape. You've got to be ready to take a punch.

STRANGE CALLS

The long count

Gene Tunney took the heavyweight crown from Jack Dempsey with a 10-round unanimous decision before 120,575 fans, Sept. 23, 1926, in Philadelphia's Sesquicentennial Stadium. The bout marked the first time a heavyweight title changed hands on a decision. When it was over, Dempsey's wife, actress Estelle Taylor, asked him what went wrong. "Honey," Dempsey said, "I forgot to duck."

The rematch and one of the most controversial bouts of all time occurred at Soldier Field in Chicago 364 days later.

But first, there was the matter of Dempsey getting by top contender Jack Sharkey. He did, but not without tumult over the seven-round decision. Dempsey savagely pounded Sharkey's body, and in the seventh, he landed a blow around the belt.

When Sharkey turned his head to protest to referee Jack O'Sullivan, Dempsey smashed his jaw with a hook, sending Sharkey down and out. The verdict stood and the stage was set for a Tunney-Dempsey rematch.

Promoter Tex Rickard, the Don King of his day, printed gold-embossed tickets. His $50 high-end ticket was the most expensive for any sporting event to date. Trains brought celebrities from all over the country to Chicago's Soldier Field. Rumors flew that Al Capone had fixed the fight, and Dempsey would win in the seventh. Boxing officials took the rumor seriously, and at the last minute replaced referee Dave Miller with Dave Barry, who had worked more than 500 fights.

A crowd of 104,943, paid a fight-record $2.6 million to watch the pugilists battle to a standoff. As it turned out, Capone nailed the round and nearly had the winner.

In the seventh, Dempsey, who had been losing the fight, unleashed a stiff left to the jaw that sent Tunney to the floor. Before the fight, during Barry's final instructions to the boxers, he reminded them of a new Illinois State Athletic Commission rule that required a fighter scoring a knockdown to go to a neutral corner. But Dempsey didn't head to a neutral corner. Instead, he walked around Barry and toward his own corner. Barry waved Dempsey away, then grabbed the boxer and shoved him. Dempsey finally realized his mistake and headed to the right spot.

Precious seconds passed before Barry started the count on Tunney.

Tunney started to make a move at the count of four. But as any championship boxer would, he remained on the canvas until the last possible moment. At the nine-count, Tunney rose to his feet. Dempsey went after him. Tunney backpedaled, danced — everything he could do to avoid Dempsey's savage blows. At one point, Dempsey waved Tunney in and said, "C'mon and fight."

Tunney quickly recovered and remained strong over the final three rounds, while Dempsey was fading. Tunney won a unanimous decision.

The Dempsey camp fumed. They lodged an official protest,

claiming Tunney got at least a 14-count. The Illinois commission backed Barry, who was the only person in the ring at that moment who was thinking straight.

Tunney offered Dempsey a second rematch, but one of the most popular boxers in history, the Manassa Mauler, declined, saying his eyesight was failing because of boxing.

The most famous of all fights is secure in boxing lore. In 1989, Tunney's victory was upheld in a mock Court of Historical Review of Appeals, a just-for-fun exercise in which the children of Tunney and Dempsey served as witnesses. John Tunney claimed his father knew exactly what he was doing by remaining on the canvas.

"The punch put him out for a second or two, but he remembered clearly looking up and picking up the referee's count at two," John Tunney said. "He always told people who asked about it, 'Yes, I could have gotten up. The only question was whether I could have gotten away, and I think I could have. I used to run backward five miles every day, so that in the event I got knocked down, I could get away.' "

Both men said the long-count controversy was the luckiest thing that ever happened to them. It kept their names in the public forum and gave added luster to both of their careers.

Olympic shame

Even before the Roy Jones, Jr. loss in the 1988 Olympics in Seoul, boxing had tainted these games and several other Olympic competitions.

In the 1964 Games at Tokyo, featherweight Vlaentin Loren took exception with his disqualification for striking his opponent with an open glove. So he belted the referee, Gyorgy Sermer of Hungary, in the face.

In the 1984 Games at Los Angeles, Evander Holyfield was disqualified from his light heavyweight semifinal after a Yugoslavian referee determined he had floored New Zealander Kevin Barry after the ref had yelled, "stop." Replays confirmed the referee's version, but it also showed both boxers had thrown late punches.

Because Barry was a knockout victim, under Olympic rules, he couldn't fight in the championship round. Therefore, the gold medal automatically went to the other semifinal winner, a Yugoslavian. The referee had to be escorted from the arena.

In the 1924 Games in Paris, a British referee disqualified an Italian boxer, Guisseppi Oldani, for holding. The Italian contingent attacked the referee with sticks, coins and other debris until a group of boxers and wrestlers came to his rescue.

Which brings us to 1988. The ugliness began soon after the Seoul Games opened. Referee Keith Walker of New Zealand was attacked by coaches, trainers and officials of the host nation after he penalized South Korean bantamweight Byun Jong-il for head-butting, costing him a decision against Alexandar Hristov of Bulgaria.

After Hirstov's hand was raised in victory, South Korean coach Kim Sung-eun stormed the ring with other compatriots and attacked Walker. "They were kicking and punching and pulling my hair out," Walker said.

Police were needed to break up the brawl. In one of the memorable snapshots of the Seoul Games, Byun Jong-il staged a 67-minute sit-in after the fight, leaving the ring only after the lights were turned out.

The Koreans were widely condemned for their poor sportsmanship, an embarrassment for the host nation in an otherwise hospitable Olympics. A year later, a report by an officer in the East German secret police listed bribes paid in Seoul to steal the gold medal from American boxers. The report, filed by Karl-Heinz Wehr, said a Korean millionaire bribed senior officials of the boxing federation to fix fights in favor of the host nation. Wehr estimated 10-20 fights were fixed, with no outcome more blatantly wrong than Jones' loss to Korea's Park Si-hun.

Jones dominated the 156-pound title match, but the 3-2 judges' decision went to Si-hun. As soon as the decision was announced, an appeal was made by the U.S. Olympic committee. Nothing came of that. One of the fight judges and even Si-hun later apologized to Jones and admitted Jones was the winner.

"Of course I'm disappointed, but I never thought it was a sure thing they would award me the gold medal," Jones told the

Jacksonville, Fla., *Times-Union* in 1997. "If they did, it might open a Pandora's box for athletes who didn't think they had a fair shake in their event. I just have to accept it. Everyone knows I won it in the ring. However, 50 years from now, everyone who saw it will be gone and only the Olympic history books will be around to tell the story."

Who really won the first Indy 500?

Everyone knows Ray Harroun won the first Indianapolis 500 in 1911, averaging 74.602 miles per hour in the Marmom Wasp, right? That's what all the record books say.

Except the record books may be wrong. The winner could have been Ralph Mulford. Compelling research turned up by gumshoe Russell Jaslow has proved the record books wrong. Here's what happened:

Around the 240-mile mark, racer Joe Jagersberger lost control of his car, which smacked into the judges' stand near the pits. The judges scattered. The car continued careening down pit road. This started a four-car pileup that blocked the track. Mulford was the first to find a hole in the mess, and drove through. The remaining cars followed him.

At this point, no one was in the scoring stand. According to newspaper accounts, Harroun took the lead at the 200-mile mark. But the final results for the lap leaders indicated Harroun didn't take the lead until the 257-mile mark.

Nobody knew for certain who was leading the race at the moment. The rest of the event passed without incident, and the one-lap-remaining flag was waved at Mulford, David Bruce-Brown and Harroun in that order. The order didn't change on the final lap.

Mulford's racing team ordered its driver to take three additional safety laps, a standard procedure in those days when scoring mistakes were more prevalent. Harroun didn't take these laps, and when Mulford reached his team, Harroun had already been recognized as the winner.

Mulford's team demanded an explanation, and the American Auto Association referee A.R. Pardington said an official winner wouldn't be announced until the next day, thus beginning an Indy 500 tradition. Mulford's team claimed the scoreboard showed their car in the lead. The judges said the scoreboard was inaccurate.

Official results the following morning upheld Harroun's victory in a time of 6:41.08. Mulford was second in 6:46.46 and Bruce-Brown third. More howls of protest from the Mulford and Bruce-Brown camps followed. Mulford protested he was penalized for taking the safety laps. Judges reconvened. They closed Harroun's winning margin to about two minutes, but didn't overturn the outcome.

Jaslow suggests the ruling was related to personalities. Harroun was an Indiana native who came out of retirement to run this race. Mulford was from California. Harroun's car was provided by influential Indianapolis businessmen.

In 1969, an 85-year-old Mulford, a class act who let the matter drop after the final decision, wouldn't cry about an injustice in an interview for *Automobile Quarterly*.

"Mr. Harroun was a fine gentleman, a champion driver and a great developmental engineer. I wouldn't want him or the Indianapolis Motor Speedway to suffer embarrassment. They have publicly credited me for leading the race and each year send me something as a remembrance."

Mulford raced at Indy 10 more times, but never officially won the event.

A goal, maybe

Controversy surrounded the 1966 World Cup from the selection of the host country through the championship game. In both cases, England emerged victorious over West Germany.

Queen Elizabeth II watched from her box at London's Wembley Stadium as the teams played evenly for the first half. In the 78th minute, a German defender knocked the ball into his own net to give England a 2-1 lead. But in the 89th minute, Germany scored the tying goal to force the 30-minute overtime.

Geoffrey Hurst received a cross from Alan Ball, 11 minutes into the overtime, and blasted a shot that banged off the lower part of the top crossbar and bounced off the grass at the goal line.

However, it's not a goal unless the entire ball crosses the line.

That moment was filled with uncertainty. The Swiss referee Gottifried Dienst made no call. The Russian linesman Tofik Bakhramov gestured no goal. But Dienst wanted to talk about it. Dienst first shook his head no, then nodded yes. The goal stood.

Although the event was televised worldwide, there was no slow motion instant replay to consult. For the first time in 32 years, the host country had won the World Cup.

In 1995, Oxford University officials, using old film and modern TV techniques, proved the ball didn't completely cross the line.

The home team's path to the 1966 final survived another controversial moment. The England-Argentina quarterfinal turned ugly in the first half, when German referee Kreitlein was listening to protests from Argentine captain Antonio Rattin. Kreitlein didn't understand Spanish and later said he was only asking for an interpreter. In a stunning move, the ref motioned Rattin off the field.

Argentinean players surrounded Kreitlein, and for a moment, it appeared the team would walk off the field. Instead, Rattin left, seven minutes after the decision. Kreitlien was struck by Argentina's Pastoriza after the game, and another Argentine, Onega, spat on the match commissioner.

From the Rattin incident, the color-card system was born. While players and officials might not understand each other's language, after 1966, they knew a yellow card meant a warning or caution and a red card meant disqualification.

Hand of God

The England-Argentina match in the 1986 quarterfinals in Mexico City was intensely watched throughout the world. The Falklands Islands War between the nations was still a festering wound. The Argentines had another open wound — the loss of the World Cup quarterfinal against England 20 years earlier, after their captain, Rattin, was thrown out of the game for protesting a call. Short-handed, Argentina fought gallantly, but surrendered the game's only goal with 13 minutes remaining.

This time, the hand of God was with the Argentines.

At the 51-minute mark, Diego Armando Maradona took a chip pass near the goal. British goaltender Peter Shilton came out, but couldn't get a hand on the ball. Maradona did and slapped it into the net.

For a moment, Maradona waited for Tunisian referee Ali Bennaceur to wave off the goal. Instead, Bennaceur started running toward midfield, meaning a goal had been scored. Maradona denied his hand had punched the ball in, claiming "the hand of God," was responsible.

Moments later, Maradona scored one of the most beautiful goals in World Cup history, darting in from midfield around several defenders, juking the goaltender at the end and kicking the ball into an empty net.

A happy ending

Referee Esse Baharmast was crucified by a world media court and lived to tell about it.

That he is considered perhaps the best "soccer" referee tells you Baharmast is American. He drew the critical Brazil-Norway match that would decide the final standings in Group A of the 1998 World Cup.

The game was scoreless until the 77th minute, when Bebeto took a feed from Denilson and scored to put the Brazilians on top. Norway responded five minutes later on a goal by Tore Flo.

Then came the call that infuriated the press corps. With two minutes remaining, Baharmast whistled a penalty against Brazil for holding. Norway scored from the penalty to hand the defending World Cup champs its first loss in this event since 1990. The victory allowed Norway to advance, and coincidentally eliminated Morocco from the competition.

Brazil didn't protest the call. Baharmast went to bed that night feeling good about his game and the call. When he woke up the next morning, it seemed the whole world was against him — at least, those in the world's media. His penalty was described as "imaginary" and a "cruel injustice to Morocco."

The reporters and the rest of the world had only certain replay angles. But a Swedish TV camera saw what Baharmast did: Brazil's Junior Baiano pulling down Flo to prevent him from receiving a pass near the goal. The evidence was irrefutable.

The press ate crow and apologized. One French newspaper suggested Baharmast work games at the highest level, because he saw what 16 television angles couldn't. Baharmast shrugged off the praise. He knew he was correct all along.

The walkoff

Only once in the more than 130 years of Wimbledon has a player walked off the court because of officiating.

American Jeff Tarango had reached the third round of the 1995 singles. He had upset 15th-seed Andrei Medvedev in the second round, and he was playing some of the best tennis of his career.

In the fateful match, Tarango trailed German Alex Mronz 7-6, 3-1 and hit a serve out. Chair umpire Bruno Rebeuh overruled, saying the point should be replayed. Mronz hadn't returned the ball, so Tarango thought he should have won the point.

Tarango gave in and prepared to replay the point. Fans started to heckle him, so Tarango turned around and shouted, "Oh, shut up." Rebeuh gave him an audible obscenity ruling. Tarango, knowing he didn't shout an obscenity, blew up. He refused to play until a supervisor heard him out. Tarango's pleas didn't impress the official, who told Rebeuh to resume the match.

Tarango shouted to Rebeuh, "You're the most corrupt official in the game and you can't do that." Rebeuh slapped Tarango with a code violation for verbal abuse and awarded the point and game to Mronz. Tarango slammed a ball to the ground and shouted, "No way, that's it." He stormed off the court and into Wimbledon history.

Moments later, Tarango's wife Benedicte slapped Rebeuh at courtside. "If Jeff slaps him, he's out of the tennis tour, so I'll do it because I think somebody should do it," was Benedicte's rationale.

In a press conference afterward, Tarango unloaded on Rebeuh, claiming the umpire bragged at parties that he favored certain players in matches. Tarango's claim was supported by a former player.

Better than nothing?

On one occasion, a portion of a tennis match was played before an empty chair.

Ivan Lendl led Larry Stefanki by a set and was up 3-0 and 40-15, in the 1985 International Players Championship at Delray Beach, Fla., when Lendl hit a serve that both players thought was long. But no fault call was made which gave Lendl the game.

Stefanki protested to umpire Luigi Brambilla, "Did you see it? Answer me!"

Brambilla didn't answer and ordered Stefanki to serve. Stefanki refused, and was penalized a point. Lendl joined the fray, supporting his opponent. Brambilla called for his supervisor, but

Chapter 4

Lendl and Stefanki played six points on their own, making their own calls with the announcer updating the score.

Before the supervisor arrived, Brambilla ordered the game to be resumed at 0-15, but the players ignored him. An embarrassed Brambilla left the court. Before an empty chair, Lendl completed a 6-2, 6-0 victory.

As he left the court, Lendl gave the traditional post-match handshake to the arm of the empty chair.

Chapter 5

WHEN IT'S NOT "ONLY A GAME"

TAKING IT SERIOUSLY

Barry Mano's awareness was heightened, or assaulted, in the early 1980s during a recreational game in California. A pitcher, angered by the ump's calls, purposely fired a warm-up fast ball toward the arbiter, striking him in the head. At that moment, the umpire became a paraplegic.

Mano never dreamed when he started the National Association of Sports Officials (NASO) in 1980, battling physical abuse would become a central focus of the organization. NASO was formed with the goal of improving working conditions for officials, providing educational materials and boosting the profession. It was not designed to provide a legislative shield.

Yet NASO has accomplished this by giving officials at the high school and recreational level an avenue for reporting problems. Professional sports have their own mechanisms for dealing with abuse. NASO addresses conflicts at the amateur levels, and has successfully pressed for legislation in several states that calls for harsh penalties when officials are assaulted. The organization has led the battle to protect officials from angry athletes, coaches, parents and fans.

Doesn't current assault law provide protection for everyone, including officials? That's what Virginia politicians asked when the state's General Assembly killed sports official assault legislation. The action came shortly after a Fairfax, Va., judge ordered a player to pay $10,000 in damages to the referee he punched in the face during a men's adult league game. The player was angry because the official had ejected a teammate for fighting. Yet, a Virginia legislator said she had a problem with a law that would jail parents for grabbing an official to get his attention during one of her kid's soccer games.

"That's exactly why the legislation is needed," Mano asserted. "Think of a sports official as a judge and the field as a court of law. Justice is presumed blind, and judgments are based on an official's, or judge's, interpretation of the rules, or law. As a condition of the event, both sides have agreed to abide by the rulings. Appeals, or written protests, are permitted, but in sports, outcomes are rarely altered."

There is one major difference between the courtroom and ball field. Decisions of law can take weeks. Decisions on the field must be made immediately and forcefully. Reactions can be just as immediate and forceful.

"If you're in the courtroom and suddenly a defendant goes after a judge and starts beating him up, what kind of outrage would that cause?" asked Mano. "It should be the same for an official. When NASO started, we got calls about abuse. But in the last three or four years, there's been an explosion. We get at least one call a week about abuse."

Every official at every level of competition has dealt with the nightmare of verbal abuse or the threat of violence — the "kill the ump" mentality. When abuse crosses the line to assault, there's more at stake than a police report. The safe environment that allows an official to confidently carry out his duties has been violated, and the sport itself loses. When abuse happens at the lowest levels of amateur sports — youth and recreation leagues — the damage can run deeper than jail time and a fine.

According to a 1987 study, youth sports experts estimated 15-20 percent of parents behave abusively toward umpires and officials at their children's sports events. Theories abound for such behavior: Parents taking out their workplace frustrations at the ball yard, an obsession with winning even though it's much less important to the children, and the influence of television.

A child who is hit by a pitch might think charging the mound is the prescribed response, because television highlight packages never show the occasions where a batter gets plunked but doesn't charge. Those ball field outbursts make for entertaining clips, but distort the lessons young players should be learning about sports. Being hit by a pitch, or an argument between the player or coach and an official is an opportunity to resolve a conflict, and can be a part of the contest. Fighting or screaming vulgarities is not. Parents don't seem to understand such aggressive behavior destroys the fun for kids.

"What are we telling our children who see adults, their parents or coaches, attack an official?" Mano aked. "We send the message that when you disagree with an authority figure, it's all right to push or throw a punch. We have young athletes who take matters into their own hands. I think, in many of these cases, they're kids who have heard 'yes' throughout their lives. When an official tells them 'no', they deal with it through abuse."

NASO has collected cases on every level. Perhaps the following litany of recent events made your local news:

• In 1998, two football players in a 140-pound Maryland league were charged with second-degree assault for throwing their helmets and hitting a referee in the back of the head. The players had already been ejected from the game for unsportsmanlike conduct. The team was disbanded.

• A Pennsylvania couple teamed up to assault a basketball referee they thought was picking on their son during a 1998 basketball game. The player fouled out early in the fourth quarter. After the game, the player's mother took a swing at the ref. The father moved the mother out of the way and also took a swing.

• A Washington high school wrestler head-butted an official and knocked him unconscious for 30 seconds after a match. The wrestler was charged with fourth-degree assault.

• In 1997, a Philadelphia high school basketball player punched a referee who had ejected him from the game after the player picked up two technical fouls in the first quarter. The player said he was frustrated when he was called for traveling after his legs were cut out from under him while going up for a lob pass. After the player showered and changed his clothes, he was arrested and led out of the gym in handcuffs.

- A New Mexico high school football player slammed into the back of a referee after he was ejected from a 1997 game for unsportsmanlike conduct. He was charged with aggravated battery on a school official.

- An Alabama umpire was held to the ground and kicked in the head by the coach of a youth baseball team in 1997.

- Officials working a 1998 high school football playoff game in Alabama were punched and pulled to the ground by fans incited by a public address announcer who said the officials "need to go back to school."

- A group of adults cheered as a New York ice hockey player punched a referee in a 1998 postgame attack. The coach had to pull the player off of the official after seven or eight blows to the head.

- An East Coast Hockey League player, Justin McPolin, was suspended for 35 games in 1998 and 1999 for punching an official in the face. The official was trying to break up a fight.

- Umpires were caught in the middle of a fight during a baseball game for 15-year-olds that ended in a benches-clearing, stands-emptying brawl in Orlando, Fla., in 1998. Three deputy sheriffs were needed to regain control.

- In 1998, a Sturgeon Bay, Wisc., Little League arbiter was punched by an assistant coach who thought the opposing pitcher committed a balk. After a postgame argument, the coach followed the umpire to the clubhouse and slugged him.

- A 36-year-old T-ball coach went to jail for 12 days for choking a 15-year-old umpire during a 1997 game in Oklahoma.

- A soccer official in San Francisco had part of his ear bitten off by a drunken, angry fan in 1998.

- NASO found that Florida high school officials ejected 212 players from games in 1994. By 1996, the number had jumped to 333.

NASO's files are bulging with cases that reflect a declining respect for officials and sportsmanship, a subject explored by the *Syracuse Post-Standard* and *Herald American* in a five-part 1998 series. The growing incivility on the field is a reflection of problems in society, the newspapers reported. Parents took a big hit. They instill the values. If they're confronting an official or coach, the impressionable minds of their children pick up on it. If they're more interested in watching a hockey brawl than the game, the kids notice it.

The idea of winning at all costs seems to affect all age groups. This attitude increases the pressure to win, increases the pressure on officials to be correct, and decreases the tolerance coaches, players and fans have for bad calls.

The newspaper series found even the worst displays of poor sportsmanship are tolerated by winners, especially on the professional level. There seemed to be little sense of outrage over the six-day suspension and $20,000 fine for the Bulls Dennis Rodman when he head-butted referee Ted Bernhardt in 1996. Same for the Lakers Nick Van Exel, who, while leaving the floor after he was ejected, rushed back and threw a forearm into the chest of official Ron Garretson, knocking him into the scorer's table. Van Exel was suspended for seven games and fined $25,000.

Two weeks later, Magic Johnson, the Lakers coach who had publicly denounced Van Exel's actions, shoved referee Scott Foster with his shoulder after a questionable non-call. Johnson was suspended for three games and fined $10,000.

Before 1996 ended, the Roberto Alomar-John Hirschbeck spitting incident drew national headlines, and there was one more ugly confrontation in the NBA. Charles Barkley, who has warned parents not to view him as a role model for children, and teammate Clyde Drexler of the Rockets, assaulted referee Jack Nies. Barkley was fined $7,500 and suspended for two games for poking Nies' nose, and Drexler was fined $5,000 and suspended for one game for bumping the ref.

As Art Taylor, associate director of Northeastern University's Center for the Study of Sports in Society told the Syracuse newspapers, "We've set up a situation where there doesn't seem to be any consequence so bad that you shouldn't do what you want. Have our ethical standards declined? Yes, they have declined."

Dr. Roy Askins, a psychology professor at Western Nevada State, former official and student of the profession, said there's no doubt the official isn't seen as the authority figure he once was.

"My experiences lead me to believe there has been a creeping erosion of respect for authority on the playing field," explained Askins. "I've seen softball leagues in California where it's part of the pastime to intimidate officials as much as possible for the purpose of getting a favorable call.

"The media, particularly television, must share the blame for inciting fans. When you're sitting at home watching a game on television, you're told by the announcers about the glaring errors being made in officiating, and you're thinking, 'They deserve the criticism,' " he said.

"But I'm puzzled that we rarely see a replay from the official's angle. If TV could show a play from directly behind an umpire or officials, we'd think differently about officiating." Askins continued, "I'm fascinated by the people in the booth who have no training in officiating, sitting far away from the action, with access to several angles of instant replay but not necessarily the angle of an official, yet the announcer speaks as if he can see things so clearly."

But Askins believes television and replay can benefit officiating.

"Especially that overhead camera angle," Askins said. "The outside corner has always been a tough call. I think in this case, the camera that's over home plate can serve as a useful tool at umpire camps in learning to call the corners. That angle is one of sports television's better innovations."

What's the price of abuse on the recreational and amateur levels? Roger Morningstar, a former University of Kansas basketball player who operates an activity center in Lawrence, Kan., has trouble finding young umpires to call baseball and softball leagues. Similar problems have been reported around the country.

"These kids aren't making a lot of money. They are doing it

because they love sports and want to see if officiating is something they might be interested in pursuing later in life," Morningstar said. "But we have a shortage because they don't want to come out here and get yelled at by parents all afternoon."

Mano, who's in the business of promoting his profession, also finds it discouraging when he attends youth games and sees a young official catching heat.

"We know these kids aren't doing it all for the money, so their other benefit, psychological income, goes down greatly when they're abused and berated. There was a time when, as an official, you could take great pride in knowing you're providing a service to a youngster. When was the last time you heard that?"

A HISTORY OF ABUSE

Abuse of officials has been around as long as the games themselves. In 1886, this sign hung from an outfield fence in Kansas City: "Please don't shoot the ump, he's doing the best he can."

After one college basketball game, a coach and a group of players didn't want to shoot the officials, just mangle them a little. Toward the end of a 1982 game between American University and West Chester State, referee Joe Lalli disallowed a game-ending shot by West Chester State that would have tied the game. West Chester coach Earl Voss and the players confronted Lalli and his partner, Joe Sylvester.

Lalli was pushed down. Military police with guard dogs were needed to clear the floor. Meanwhile, a West Chester player tried to gain entrance into the officials' dressing room with a crowbar.

Throughout the 1980s, baseball endured similar incidents that proved embarrassing for the NBA in 1996, beginning with Pirates third baseman Bill Madlock pushing his glove into the face of umpire Jerry Crawford. Madlock had looked at a called third strike with the bases loaded in a game against the Expos. He got his glove from another player and pushed it into Crawford's face.

Madlock downplayed the incident. "If I wanted to hit the man, I would have hit him. I pushed my glove near his face. There was no intention to hurt him."

Madlock was fined $5,000, and suspended for 15 games, which cost him $20,000 in salary. When Madlock appealed the penalty, the incident became one of the first to pit the players' union against the umpires' union. Madlock's hearing was delayed more than a month, and umpires threatened to eject him from every game he played. Five weeks after the incident, Madlock withdrew his appeal and served the suspension.

"My decision to drop the appeal at this time is based on my belief that further publicity of this matter will do a disservice not only to me, but also to the game of baseball and the Pittsburgh Pirates," Madlock said in a statement. "I am taking this action at this time in an effort to preserve the integrity of the game and to avoid any detriment to the Pittsburgh organization and my Pirate teammates."

In 1982, Orioles manager Earl Weaver was suspended for one week and fined $2,000 for striking umpire Terry Cooney. Weaver pointed his finger in Cooney's face and made contact. The incident marked the 86th ejection of his 14-year career.

In 1988, Reds manager Pete Rose was suspended for 30 days and fined $10,000 for shoving Dave Pallone in a close play at first base in which Pallone made the correct safe call, but was late. During the argument, Rose inadvertently poked Pallone in the nose, resulting in two retaliatory shoves. Pallone shoved Rose. Rose shoved Pallone.

The shower of debris became so bad that Pallone, who made the disputed call at first base in the ninth inning, ran off the field to the umpires' locker room. The game ended with three umpires.

Baseball witnessed a spitting incident during the decade, although it didn't receive the level of publicity of the Alomar-Hirschbeck episode. In 1980, Braves manager Bobby Cox admitted spitting tobacco juice on umpire Jerry Dale, but only in retaliation. "OK, I did it. I spat in his face intentionally," Cox said. "But not until he spat in my face."

The incident came in the ninth inning, when Cox argued a call by Dale at second base that prevented the Braves from completing an inning-ending double play in a loss to the Dodgers. Cox, who was ejected, said the first time he sprayed Dale with tobacco juice, "… it wasn't intentional. But then, he spat on me so I spat back. I would never spit at an umpire's face intentionally. I would never spit in anyone's face. But if a guy hits you in the jaw, you have to hit him back."

Dale's version: "Cox spat tobacco in my face and all over my shirt. He spat right in my eye the first time. I never had anyone do that. It was a disgraceful, cowardly act."

National League President Chub Feeney leveled a puny $300 fine and three-game suspension for Cox.

During the 1980s, conduct by officials and umpires became more aggressive. Not to the point of fisticuffs, but the arbiter no longer would stand with his back turned toward an arguing manager or player, accepting insults as part of the job.

When New Jersey Devils coach Jim Schoenfeld uttered his now famous, "You fat pig. Go have another doughnut," comment to ref Don Koharski, the ref defiantly shot back, "You'll never work in this league again."

Umpire Durwood Merrill once deliberately walked in the path of a Yankees pitcher who had been arguing balls and strikes through the inning. They renewed their argument and the pitcher was ejected.

In 1983, Joe West became the first umpire in baseball history to be suspended for shoving a manager when he pushed the Braves' Joe Torre. The incident occurred after an Atlanta game with Houston. Torre followed West to the umpire's dressing room to protest a called third strike on Atlanta's Bob Watson by fill-in ump Steve Ripley, the final out in a 4-3 Astros victory.

West shoved Torre because he thought the manager shouldn't have been there. West was fined $500 and suspended for three games. The fine eventually was reduced to $300; Torre was fined $200.

Chapter 5

Mad as heck and not going to take it anymore? Partly. But there's also a feeling of empowerment. By the 1980s, officials from all major sports had joined unions. They successfully fought for their rights in pay and benefits, and now were fighting against injustices and lack of respect on the field. They were no longer going to be bullied.

Chapter 6

HISTORY

THE OFFICIAL EVOLUTION

Taking charge

The concept of officiating is as old as the games themselves. Officiating evolved with the games. As the games grew, so did the need for better regulation, rules interpretation and just plain command of the situation. Some sports, like basketball, were conceived with an arbiter in mind. However, other sports evolved more slowly.

The game's inventor, James Naismith, specifically spelled out the function of the referee in his 13 original rules, penned in 1891.

"RULE 10: The umpire shall be judge of the men and shall note the fouls and notify the referee when three consecutive fouls have been made. He shall have the power to disqualify men according to Rule 5 (which specifically prohibited shouldering, holding, pushing, tripping or striking an opponent. If a player intentionally injured an opponent, he was gone for the remainder of the game and the team had to play short-handed).

"RULE 11: The referee shall be judge of the ball and shall decide when the ball is in play, in bounds, to which side it belongs and shall keep the time. He shall decide when a goal has been made, and shall keep account of the goals, along with any other duties performed by the referee."

Naismith invented the game as an indoor wintertime diversion. Although his early games sometimes included 20 on a side, he deplored rough play. Naismith would have preferred no contact at all, but he understood that wasn't an option.

He not only was the game's inventor, Naismith was its first referee. He spent his last 40 years coaching and teaching at the University of Kansas. As the Jayhawks first coach, Naismith felt his duty wasn't to win games, but to teach basketball. When he accompanied Kansas on road trips, he often called the game.

That wasn't the case for Alexander Cartwright, the bank clerk who founded the New York Knickerbocker Base Ball Club in 1845. Baseball's first rules were written that year. They included a provision that the team president "shall appoint an Umpire, who shall keep the game in a book provided for that purpose, and note all violations of the Bylaws and Rules. All disputes and differences relative to the game will be determined by the Umpire, from which there is no appeal." In the earliest games, the umpire didn't call balls or strikes, and batters had to swing and miss three pitches to be out. An attorney, William R. Wheaton, officiated the first recorded game October 6, 1845.

At first, the umpires' input was rarely sought. The ump sat at a table along the third base line. On occasion, the umpire was a town's honored citizen and was not paid for his services. If he was feeling proper that day, he'd wear a top hat and tails. An arbiter only settled disputes, and then, he met with both teams' captains before announcing a decision. In the spirit of fair play, he might even consult with spectators closest to the action. Above all, the umpire was a gentleman.

Of course, that didn't last long. The practice of consulting with fans ended by 1880, when the umpire was on the field. In 1878, the two-year-old National League instructed its clubs to pay umpires $5 per game, and a year later, the NL composed the game's first list, or staff, of umpires from which teams could choose.

By then, baseball had developed a rowdy side. Owners did little to stop the growing violence against umpires, who often needed a police escort to leave the field. Fans' freedom to cuss, spit and throw objects at umpires was good for the box office. Author Benjamin Rader, in his book, *Baseball*, describes one arbiter who fought back. His name was Robert Ferguson.

"Angered by the 'growling' of (New York) Mutuals catcher Robert Hicks, Ferguson grabbed a bat and broke the offender's arm in two places. He thereby disabled Hicks for the rest of the game. At the game's conclusion, a constable stepped forward to arrest Ferguson, but the injured catcher refused to press charges."

Overall, umpires of the 1880s and 1890s suffered great abuse. In the final years of the 19th century, baseball was played with a violent streak and it wasn't unusual for a dispute to end with an ump exchanging blows with a player or manager. Tim Keefe walked away from the profession in the middle of the 1895 season because "... it is the fashion now for every player to froth at the mouth and emit shrieks of anguish whenever a decision is given which is adverse to the interest of his club."

The aggravation hardly seemed worth the paltry salary. In the early 1880s, the American Association paid its umpires $140 per month, and required them to wear blue coats and caps. Moreover, the arbiters had little authority. The 1885 season-ending series between Chicago and St. Louis ended in a 3-3-1 draw. St. Louis pulled its team off the field in the second game after feuding with umpire Dave Sullivan, who declared Chicago the winner by forfeit.

The next four games went off without a hitch, but with a new arbiter. Before the seventh game, Chicago, leading the series, agreed not to accept the forfeited victory. But after St. Louis won the seventh game, Chicago insisted the forfeit counted, leaving the series dead even.

A year earlier, one of the games in the season-ending series between Providence and New York was officiated by a Providence player.

The players had the upper hand, and weren't afraid to use it across an umpire's face. James Lincoln made his debut and ended his career as an umpire in 1913. After being verbally abused by New York Giants players during a game, he found himself surrounded by the angry players afterward. They shoved and spiked Lincoln, who quit that day.

Then along came an arbiter that changed the profession, or at least the perception of the profession. Bill Klem rapidly worked his way up the ladder, from umpiring town team games in Pennsylvania to the Connecticut League, New York State League and the American Association in just two years. Before he worked one game in the top minor league, Klem had caught the eye of National League President Harry Pulliam.

Klem made his major league debut in 1905, at a time when "... an umpire's life wasn't worth a nickel and in those days, he often finished his day's labor with a hurried sprint to the fence and jumped over it," according to a *Sporting News* article. He was hired for $2,100 a year, and in his first six weeks on the job, Klem tossed out 30 players and managers.

Klem retired after the 1940 season. When he died in 1951, Klem was hailed as the best umpire of all time. As a tribute to his greatness, he was asked to work the most important game of the baseball season only three years into his major league career — the Giants-Cubs playoff game in 1908.

Klem's willingness to stand up to an irate manager or player won him respect throughout baseball. Some of the early stories that built Klem's reputation came in the minor leagues. In one of his first games, Klem fined the league secretary for jawing from a dugout.

During an American Association game, Klem, working from a position behind the pitcher as a lone official, drew the ire of the center fielder/manager, who charged in to argue the strike zone.

With his toe, Klem drew an imaginary line behind the mound, turned around and started walking toward the plate. The player reached the line, stopped and glared at Klem before retreating to his position. Klem later said he relied on intuition to defuse the situation. He frequently pulled the same stunt in the majors.

"The secret was turning my back on the player after drawing the line," Klem told *The Sporting News*. "If I had drawn the line, stood there and tried to out-stare and out-argue the rowdy, it wouldn't have worked. He no doubt would have accepted it as an act of defiance and crossed the line. But when he had only my back to stare at, it had a curious psychological effect on him. That little trick made me an umpire. I drew that line on a lot of great players in the National League, and it always worked."

A manager once tried to upstage Klem. Brooklyn manager Leo Durocher charged Klem early in a game. Klem drew his line. Then Durocher drew one of his own and started kicking dirt all over it. Klem leaned against the grandstand until Durocher was finished and play resumed.

"An arrogant little autocrat with confidence in both his ability and infallibility," is how Arthur Daley of *The New York Times* described Klem.

As you may suspect, Klem took no guff, even from the game's stars. When baseball began incorporating two umpires in the early 1900s, Klem didn't rotate positions, as was customary — he once went 16 years without working the bases. He was almost exclusively a home-plate umpire with the utmost confidence in the strike zone. Although he missed a play at first every now and then, he never called a strike wrong, as he once told a player.

"You young punk. I called strikes and balls before you were born and a lot of smart people seemed to be satisfied. Now a busher like you has the gall to ask me, 'Bill Klem, do you think it missed the corner?' No, it didn't miss the corner. If it had, I'd have said, 'Ball.' "

Klem once got the better of legendary Giants manager John McGraw regarding the point of impact of a foul ball. The Polo Grounds scoreboard cut across the foul line on the outfield wall. The line started at the bottom of the scoreboard, jumped over the numbers and continued at the top. During a game, a Giants player smacked a ball off the wall where the foul line was missing, and Klem called it foul. McGraw flew into a rage. The next day, McGraw instructed a groundskeeper to inspect the dent in the scoreboard and discovered Klem's call was correct by three inches. "Naturally," Klem said confidently. "I never missed one in my life."

Klem ruled absolutely. During a 1911 game between Cincinnati and St. Louis, he struck Cardinals manager Roger Bresnahan, one of the feistiest managers ever. A group of Cincinnati businessmen paid Klem's $50 fine.

He knew the rule book backward and forward, but he also knew when to veer from the prescribed. One afternoon at the Polo Grounds, the Giants were riding Klem by calling him "Catfish." Just before the Boston Braves batted in the sixth, Klem removed his mask, looked into the Giants' dugout and shouted, "All of you guys get off the field, quick. I don't know which one of you is guilty, so you all go!" The non-starters marched through right field to the clubhouse.

Giants pitcher Chief Meyers said the Giants often pushed the automatic ejection button.

" ... all you had to do was call him 'Catfish,' and out of the game you'd go," Meyers said in *The Glory of Their Times.* "That's all. Just that one word, and you were out. I'm not quite sure why. Maybe it was because he had rather prominent lips, and when he'd call a ball or a strike, he'd let fly a rather fine spray from his mouth. Sort of gave the general impression of a catfish, you know. He was a little sensitive about it."

Tigers outfielder Goose Goslin made that mistake during the 1934 World Series. Goslin, an American Leaguer, had only heard stories about Klem's wrath. He felt it the next day in a hotel elevator when Klem lectured him in the lobby. Commissioner Landis fined Klem $50 for his outburst and had it deducted from his World Series check. Klem returned the check. It went back and forth for a year.

That incident, plus an admission to Landis that he wagered on horse racing, cost Klem assignments in the World Series from 1935-1939. But he ended his career in the spotlight, calling the 1940 series between the Reds and Tigers.

Klem revolutionized umpiring. He was the first to leave his position to get a better angle, sprinting from base to base in the days when only one or two umpires worked a game. He was also among the first to give visual definition to calls, sweeping his arms on foul balls and drawing back the thumb on an "out" call. He demanded respect. He asked to be called "Mister," by managers and players, and he returned the courtesy.

One of his most famous decisions was a non-call. During the 1911 World Series between the Giants and Athletics, New York's Larry Doyle came home on a sacrifice fly in the 10th inning. But Doyle never touched the plate. Nor did catcher Jack Lapp apply a tag. Both teams left the field assuming the winning run had scored for a 4-3 New York victory. Klem stood motionless at the plate as the teams left the field. Klem issued the following statement later that evening: "Had Lapp or any Athletic tagged Doyle before the New York player left the park, I would have had to call Larry out for the third out. As it was too dark to start another inning, I would have called (the game) a 3-3 tie. But it was not up to me to call the attention of Lapp or any other Athletic players to the fact that Doyle hadn't touched the plate."

Klem was so revered, baseball took notice of his lifetime of achievements. During his career, Klem called more than 5,000 games and 18 World Series. In 1939, Klem received a plaque from the New York chapter of the Baseball Writer's Association of America for "meritorious service to baseball over a long period." In 1949, the Giants paid tribute with "Bill Klem Night" at the Polo Grounds, where he was showered with gifts.

Naturally, the popular Klem had his detractors. Former National League umpire Beans Reardon once claimed Klem tried to assert his influence with other umpires when he advocated a new rule stating all NL umps should use the inside chest protector. Reardon preferred the outside protector, which was popular in the American League.

Klem was elected to the Hall of Fame in 1953, along with fellow umpire Tom Connolly, his quiet counterpart from the American League.

After serving three years in the National League, Connolly switched to the upstart AL in its inaugural season — 1901. His assignment on Opening Day was Cleveland at Chicago. Because the other three American League games were rained out that day, Connolly holds the distinction of umpiring the AL's first game.

Connolly racked up a series of firsts in his career. He called the opening games at Philadelphia's Shibe Park (1909), old Comiskey Park (1910) in Chicago, Boston's Fenway Park (1912) and Yankee Stadium (1923). Connolly and Hank O'Day of the National League called the first World Series in 1903. Only two umpires called each World Series from 1903-1908, then two were added to the staff in 1909 and eventually, two more.

Although small in stature at 5'7", Connolly was tough. He once tossed Babe Ruth. But ejecting players and managers wasn't his style. He went 10 straight seasons without giving the thumb. Rather, Connolly tried to help the younger players. For instance, opponents were riding future Hall-of-Famer Eddie Plank in his major league debut in 1901. "Son, from what you have shown me today, you'll be here a long time," Connolly said. "I'll take care of that crew in the dugout."

Following Klem and Connolly into the Hall of Fame from the early years were three outstanding umps, including Jocko Conlan, who also broke ranks with Klem by wearing an outside protector. Also inducted was Billy Evans, an American Leaguer from 1906-1927, who once had a fistfight with Ty Cobb under the stands in Washington. Players had to separate them. Finally, Bill McGowan, the original iron man, who called every inning of 2,541 consecutive games beginning in 1925.

However, McGowan's temper got the better of him in 1948, when he threw a ball-and-strike indicator at a Senators pitcher. He found himself in hot water again a few years later when he refused to tell St. Louis reporters which Tigers players he ejected for taunting Browns pitcher Satchel Paige.

Paige, who played for more than 20 Negro League teams throughout his career, was one of the game's finest control pitchers. Even in its heyday years of the 1920s, the Negro League couldn't afford traveling umpires, so each team provided its own. Joe Rue, an American League arbiter from 1938-47, got his start calling Monarchs games in Kansas City and recalled that all the umpires he saw in the Negro League's earliest years were white.

Other key dates and historic firsts in the umpire evolution:

1871 J.L. Boake umpires the first professional league game.

1876 Billy McLean umpires the first National League game.

1903 Hank O'Day and Tommy Connolly call the first World Series.

1912 The two-umpire system becomes standard and the AL and NL each have 10-man staffs. Two for each game and two reserves.

1917 Klem receives $1,000 for working the World Series.

1933 Three umpires regularly were assigned to games.

1933 Bill Dinneen, Bill Klem, Cy Rigler and Bill McGowan umpire the first All-Star Game at Comiskey Park.

1935 First umpire training school opened by NL umpire George Barr.

1952 The four-man crew becomes standard.

1953 Bill Klem and Tommy Connolly are first umpires enshrined in the Hall of Fame.

1966 Emmett Ashford becomes the major league's first black umpire.

1974 Armando Rodriguez becomes the major's first Hispanic umpire.

Nobody wins this race

The paucity of black umpires in the earliest days of the Negro League, which started in 1920, was a source of contention within the black community. In 1921, Negro National League Founder and President Rube Foster attempted to explain the condition in *The Chicago Defender* and *The Kansas City Call.*

"The leading thinkers of this country today admit it was cruel and unjust for four million slaves, uneducated and ignorant, to be turned loose as a free people without safeguarding the necessary things in life for them — preparing and fitting them for the duties necessary as citizens and free people. These same conditions confront baseball as far as the umpires of the race are concerned."

Foster reasoned that while blacks had been playing baseball for decades, very few black umpires had been trained, and those used weren't respected by the players. *The Chicago Defender* didn't buy it, and railed against white umpires in its editorial columns. Letters of support poured in. Let black umpires learn on the job, they suggested. Foster gave in. The 1923 season opened with seven black umpires in the Negro National League. For the record, they were Billy Donaldson, B.E. Gholston, Leon Augstine, Lucian Snaer, Caesar Jamison, William Embry and Tom Johnson.

But the umps had trouble taking control of games. Gholston quit in 1925 and spoke for a frustrated and dispirited bunch.

"Several teams of the National Negro League are still under the impression that they shouldn't take orders from colored umpires," Gholston wrote in *The Kansas City Call.* "Several threatened to jump on the umpires. The colored umpires have two battles to fight and both of them are hard: We are willing to struggle for recognition in competition with the white umpires, but it hurts to have to fight for the respect of members of our own race and league, from the president down to the bat boy."

Gholston kept attacking Foster. The accusations included: Favoritism of umpires from his Chicago hometown, not supporting two umpires who were struck by players, not honoring contracts that called for annual raises (salaries were frozen at $142 a month for three seasons) and firing a number of umpires while they were on the road, but not compensating them for a return trip home.

By the end of the 1925 season, none of the original black umpires were working in the Negro National League. What's more, no black umpires worked the first Negro World Series in 1924. Foster, who organized the event, dipped into the minor leagues for signal callers.

How bad was it in the Negro Leagues? Players recalled umpires were under pressure to help the home team.

"The umpire stood behind me, not behind the catcher. Every time I got ready to pitch, he'd yell, 'Ball!'" said pitcher Dolittle Young in *Kansas City Monarchs, Champions of Black Baseball.* "I said, 'Just wait 'til I throw the ball, then you can call it a ball. Now the next one you call a ball, I'm going to get on you.' I drawed back to throw and he called a ball. I reached down, got a double handful of sand and put it down his collar. He took me out of the game. I sure was glad, because it was hot out there."

Smoothing football's rough edges

The original football officials served a similar function to the early baseball umpires. They weren't on the field to call penalties, but to settle arguments between the teams. The earliest games, primarily involving Northeastern colleges, were officiated on the honor system. Each side had an arbiter, with the traveling team bringing its own. The game also had a referee, whose job was to settle disagreements between umpires. The umpires were often chosen for their debate skills, rather than their knowledge of the game.

From the game called "football's first" — the 1869 contest between Rutgers and Princeton — until a major overhaul of the regulations in 1906, the rules governing each football game varied. For that first game, the ball could be kicked and head-butted, but not carried. When the ball was caught in the air or on the first bounce, a free kick was permitted. There were 25 men per team.

For the next three decades, the rules struggled to catch up with the game. As with Naismith in basketball, football's top coaches often served as officials. Walter Camp was the ref for the 1879 Princeton-Harvard game. In 1885, he officiated the Yale-Princeton contest and ruled against his alma mater, allowing a controversial touchdown to stand in Princeton's one-point victory. Camp was so highly regarded as an official, he was asked by Harvard to call the 1886 Harvard-Yale contest.

Camp became Yale's coach in 1888 and enjoyed a Hall of Fame career. The American Intercollegiate Football Rules Committee paid him the ultimate tribute upon his death in 1925. "If football is to continue as the greatest of all academic sports, it will be due not alone to the foundations, toward the building of which Walter Camp contributed so generously, but in a far greater measure to the fine standards of American sportsmanship, toward the establishment of which no man in America has contributed more, either by precept or by example."

Amos Alonzo Stagg and Pop Warner also called games. Why not? They may not have invented their sport, but they knew it better than anyone else.

However, the influence of the game's great coaches couldn't keep the sport from spiraling to near extinction in the first years of the 20th century. Football was getting ugly, deadly. Not even a meeting in 1894 among the top teams — Harvard, Yale, Penn and Princeton along with a top official, Paul Dashiell of Navy — could hammer out enough new rules to keep the game safe. The changes included: eliminating the flying wedge (a reverse V-shaped formation of blockers to protect the ball carrier on kickoff returns) which was killing players, reducing playing time from 90 to 70 minutes, and adding a third official to the crew of one umpire and a referee.

Despite these efforts, football became rougher and college presidents were fed up. Harvard and Yale stopped playing between 1895-1897, after an especially fierce 1894 contest.

Then came 1905, the year football almost ceased to exist. The game's death toll of 18, with 159 serious injuries, shocked the nation and President Teddy Roosevelt. Columbia, Northwestern, California and Stanford all suspended the sport. Football was revived at a 1906 meeting in New York.

Among the rules established was the addition of a second arbiter and increasing the on-field officials to four. Another rule required substitutions to report first to the referee. Finally, the legalization of the forward pass ended the mass plays responsible for countless injuries.

Football didn't lend itself to the colorful characters of baseball and basketball. But there were football officiating pioneers, including Mike Thompson, who called games around the turn of the century. Among his contributions to the profession was the practice of asking coaches before a game if they were planning to run any unusual plays. Hey, it was the 1900s. New plays were created weekly. Thompson just wanted to ensure that teams stayed within the rules, what few there were.

In 1903, Thompson worked a game between Princeton and Carlisle, the school Jim Thorpe made famous a few years later. That day, Carlisle coach Pop Warner told Thompson he was going to spring a hidden-ball trick. But the game was played in a downpour, so Warner kept his trick in the bag.

However, the following week, Carlisle traveled to Harvard and the weather was ideal. The Crimson scored the first touchdown and kicked off to the Indians. Jimmy Johnson of Carlisle caught the ball, and before heading upfield tucked into his V-wedge formation, he placed the ball under the back of the sweater of his teammate, Dillon, who was standing behind him, facing Carlisle's end zone.

"The V-wedge immediately was in motion toward Harvard, with Johnson inside, drawing all the Harvard team," Thompson wrote in 1931. "As the first of the Crimson impact met the wedge, Dillon detached himself and eased toward the sideline, traveling slowly until he was clear. When Harvard finally brought the wedge down in a heap, one of the Indians fell with what appeared to be the ball in his arms, but it was actually his headgear. All of Harvard piled on top of him.

"Meanwhile, I was shadowing Dillon down the field. Once in the clear, he broke into a dead run, with me flying behind him. The Harvard team ignored us, and many of the 25,000 spectators thought I was chasing Dillon off the field for some infraction of the rules. When a few fans detected the bulging lump on his back and guessed what was up, a hum arose in the crowd that grew into a roar.

"When Dillon crossed the Harvard goal line, he threw himself down on his back. 'Down yet, Mike? Down yet, Mike?' he kept calling. Here was a pretty problem. The rules said the ball must be grounded. Was a ball grounded when a jersey intervened between it and the soil?

"Dillon could not reach the ball with his hands, but Jimmy Johnson saved me from this dilemma. He had detached himself from the heap and followed us downfield. He reached under Dillon's sweater, snatched the ball, and grounded it. Though Dillon had always been credited with that touchdown, Johnson actually made it."

Naturally, Harvard coaches were ticked off. In those days, the forward pass was illegal, and they thought Johnson putting the ball in Dillon's sweater constituted a pass. But as Thompson explained, Dillon was standing behind Johnson when the exchange was made. Incidentally, Dillon was wearing a large rubber band around his body so the ball wouldn't slip out.

Thompson went on to write that later in the season, he worked a game in the South where the punt return team attempted a variation of the hidden-ball trick. This time, the return man received the punt, took out a knife, slit the ball from end to end and put the deflated pigskin on his head. As the player headed up field, Thompson blew the whistle.

" 'You let the Indians get away with it,' the coach yelled at me,"

Thompson wrote. "But I replied, 'Do you know the first rule in the book? Look it up.' The first rule specifies that the ball shall be a tightly inflated oblate spheroid."

Regarding officials, pro football followed the same lines as the college game. In 1947, the pro game increased its ranks from four to five officials. It added a sixth in 1965 and a seventh in 1978. Perhaps the best-known person in officiating circles in the early years wasn't an official — it was Hugh "Shorty" Ray.

He stood only 5'6", and worked full-time as a mechanical drawing instructor at Harrison High School in Chicago. But Ray was so influential, he was elected to the Pro Football Hall of Fame in 1966.

Ray was considered one of the best officials in the Big Ten when Bears coach George Halas recommended the NFL hire him. Ray served as the game's technical adviser from 1938-1956. Essentially, he was the officials' official. He held clinics, tested officials, mailed announcements, and pounded the rules into their heads.

During games, Ray was the first to grade officials from the press box. He and his assistants carried watches, clipboards and pencils to record every move. On those occasions when he couldn't field a crew, Ray broke down the film.

Ray kept running totals. At the end of each season, he presented his conclusions at league meetings. Every play had been recorded.

Because of Ray's recommendations, the NFL revised its rules on long incompletions. Previously, an official ran back with the ball.

However, Ray suggested a person on the sidelines hand a second ball to the referee to save time.

Containing hoops hysteria

Basketball's popularity spread rapidly in the 1890s. Several schools claimed to have played the first five-man game, but the first public berating of officials came in a student newspaper report of a January 16, 1896, game at Iowa City, Iowa. The University of Chicago beat Iowa 15-12. According to one account, the strict officiating was "a source of great dissatisfaction to the audience."

Conferences had not yet been formed, but the public and press were already bagging the officials. Like the early going in baseball and football, early hoops could be a blood sport. Initially, when a ball rolled out of bounds, it was given to the first team that touched it out of bounds, not the last to touch it before it crossed the line. Players battled in mad scrambles to slap at the ball. When the ball landed in the balcony, teams fought each other up a stairway or devised a way to hoist themselves up.

Officiating was always part of the game, as Naismith's rules demanded, but so were the indignities arbiters suffered at the hands of the fans. Indeed, officials knew which windows in their locker rooms were unlocked, or they unlocked them, in anticipation of beating a hasty retreat.

In sharp contrast to today's disciplined, business-like approach to officiating, early basketball referees were as much a spectator attraction as the players. Officials like Pat Kennedy, Ernie Quigley, Jim Enright and Lou Bello would play to the crowd. There was also a ref named Chuck Soladare, who had no teeth. He'd gum his calls. These arbiters believed they were part of the price of admission, like a Globetrotters official. Kennedy, in fact, worked with that troupe for seven years.

On one occasion, while working a professional game, Kennedy called a foul on a player for praying on the court. The player had clasped his hands and was begging for a call.

According to legend, Ernie Quigley once told a coach he wouldn't be assessed a technical foul for rushing onto the court, but the opponent would be allowed to shoot a free throw for every step it took the coach to return to the bench. However, Quigley was outfoxed later in the season when he made a similar threat to another coach, but the coach summoned two players to the floor to carry him back to the bench.

During a 1946 game, Enright gave a Notre Dame player four free throws on a hard foul by a Butler player. That wasn't the original plan, but the Irish player kept missing, and Enright wanted him to make one.

A distinctive uniform was first suggested by the rules makers in 1917. Former Kentucky coach Adolph Rupp, who called games in his native Kansas during those years, remembered ducking passes when the white or blue shirt he was wearing matched the color of a team's jersey.

As the game's popularity grew in the 1920s and 1930s, it became evident that the rules varied, depending on the part of the country in which the game was played. Rupp recalled a 1935 game at Madison Square Garden when the Wildcats lost to New York University by a point.

Kentucky had the ball and was leading in the final seconds, when an official called an offensive foul on a pick. Picks had never been called as fouls in the South or Midwest, but it sent NYU to the line for the winning free throws. Only a year earlier, basketball rules were standardized, but several seasons would pass before the entire country would be operating on the same page.

A group of top college officials, including Pat Kennedy, moved to the pro game when the NBA forerunner, the Basketball Association of America, was formed in 1946. Officials, earning only $30-40 per game, soon learned the pro fans weren't as civilized as college fans. Syracuse could be a particularly tough town.

Former NBA great Sid Borgia recalled the night he and John Nucatola had to be escorted off the floor by six policemen as irate fans tried to punch them. They had to send for their clothes because a mob was waiting for them back at the hotel. Borgia also remembered the night a fan rushed out of the stands and attacked him. Borgia punched out most of the man's teeth.

"It used to be, when we called a technical foul against the home team, the public address announcer couldn't wait to tell everyone," Borgia recalled. "We would be showered with debris for 15 minutes. It was so bad, I must have had as many police escorts as the top scorers in the league."

There is one area yesterday's officials have in common with

today's: they work their tails off. Some of today's college officials are accused of working too often. Three games in three days in three time zones are not unheard of. But their forefathers did the same thing. Kennedy related that when he broke into officiating, during an average week, he would work six recreational games, two afternoon school games and two pro games on Sunday.

Pucks, kicks and brawls

The first rules of ice hockey were recorded in 1898, although the game had been around since at least 1875. Formulation of the original rules is credited to J.G.A. Creighton, a native of Halifax, Nova Scotia.

Creighton came up with only a handful of rules, as hockey developed slowly. The face-off was invented by a turn-of-the-century official, Fred C. Waghorne. In those days, a game was started by an official arranging the puck between two players' sticks. He would then take a blade in each hand and place them against the puck. The ref would quickly retreat and yell, "Play", but he was often banged in the shin in the process.

Waghorne decided he'd been clubbed enough and was the first to drop the puck.

According to *The Hockey Encyclopedia,* "supervision of the early matches was casual."

In 1898, only a referee and two goal officials were required. Until the 1930s, the home team selected the officials and a visiting coach or general manager could request a change. A request for a change of officials actually happened between the third and fourth games of the 1938 Stanley Cup Finals, when Toronto Maple Leafs manager Conn Smythe demanded the replacement of the entire crew.

When the NHL formed in 1917, the rules called for a referee and an assistant when necessary. The assistant had the same powers as a ref. The linesman was introduced in 1926, only a few days after a referee was forced to stop a game laced with brutality between the Boston Bruins and Montreal Maroons.

In 1933, the NHL added a "judge of play" to the lineup, which was essentially a second referee. Each official handled one half of the ice. Two years later, the league required the referees switch sides during the game. The system lasted until the 1937-38 season, when the linesman replaced the second referee.

Eventually, a game crew consisted of a referee, two linesmen on ice, an official scorer, game timekeeper, penalty timekeeper and two goal judges.

Like hockey and other sports, soccer often allowed its earliest participants to police themselves with a gentlemanly code of conduct. At important matches between English public schools, each team supplied an umpire, but the early rules did not require a game to be played with an official.

Developed in 1867, Cheltenham College of Rules was the first set of regulations to call for officials. Each side would choose an arbiter. The umpires would select a referee, whose job was to settle arguments between umpires.

In 1880, the duties of umpires were spelled out in the *Official*

Laws of the Game:

"By mutual consent of the competing clubs, a referee shall be appointed whose duty shall be to decide all disputes between umpires. He shall also keep a record of the game and act as timekeeper, and in the event of ungentlemanly behaviour on the part of any contestants, the offender or offenders shall, in the presence of the umpires, be cautioned. In the case of violent conduct, the referee shall have the power to rule the offending player or players out of play, and order him or them off the ground, transmitting the name or names to the committee of the Association under whose rules the game was played, and in whom shall be solely vested the right of accepting an apology."

In 1891, umpires were replaced with linesmen. By 1894, the referee moved onto the field from the sidelines and wielded absolute authority over the game.

Soccer had been an Olympic sport since 1900, so international competition was well established when the World Cup debuted in 1930. Because of the game's wild popularity, along with an emotional final between home-standing Uruguay and fellow South American Argentina, World Cup officials decided not to risk the personal safety of the title game official by releasing his name ahead of time.

John Langenus of Belgium wasn't announced as the referee until just three hours before the game, and Langenus didn't take any chances. He demanded special protection for himself and his assistants and security guards for his family. He also arranged for a boat to whisk him and his family away no later than one hour after the match.

Fortunately, there were no major incidents as Uruguay won, 4-2, before a throng of 90,000. Ironically, Langenus changed professions to journalism for the 1934 World Cup in Italy. When the host defeated Spain 1-0 on a controversial goal in the quarterfinals, Langenus cried foul in his article.

An umpire was identified in boxing's first set of guidelines, *Broughton's Boxing Rules of 1743*. Rule VI: "To prevent disputes, in every main battle the principals shall, on coming on the stage, choose from among the gentlemen present two Umpires, who shall absolutely decide all disputes that may arise about the battle; and if the two Umpires cannot agree, the said Umpires will chose a third, who is to determine it."

WOMEN WITH WHISTLES

Baseball and basketball

A great triumph for women officials was lost when Bernice Gera, after three years of litigation, became the first female to umpire a professional baseball game in 1972. But she quit her job after the first game of a doubleheader in the New York-Penn rookie league following a heated argument with a manager.

There have been many victories since, but none surpassed the historic 1997 announcement that Dee Kantner and Violet Palmer would become the first women to work NBA regular season games — the first women to work the regular season of any major league sport.

Kantner and Palmer were considered top college officials — the two best in the WNBA. Kantner, 37 when she was hired, worked as the league's supervisor, called NBA summer league games for three years, preseason games for two, officiated in all the major college conferences in the East and Midwest and worked four NCAA women's title games.

Palmer, four years younger than Kantner, had similar NBA experience. She worked the major conferences in the West and Midwest and in four women's Final Fours.

Their road to the NBA started more than a decade earlier, when the league's eyes were opened to female referees calling women's games during the 1984 Olympics in Los Angeles. The late Darlene May became the first woman to officiate Olympic basketball. May, who died in 1996 of breast cancer, coached the women's basketball team at Cal Poly Pomona while Palmer was a point guard there. Then-NBA Officials Supervisor Darell Garretson noticed May, and the seed was planted for women to join the league.

Fate also played a role. In 1988, the NBA increased its staff from two to three per game, and phased in an additional 25 referees during a two-year period. The staff grew from 30-35 to 55-60. Before the 1997-98 season, the NBA found itself with five openings, when one retired and four others were indicted for tax fraud.

Kantner and Palmer, who first had been contacted by the NBA in 1995, worked league-sponsored summer leagues for three years. They weren't hired to deflect attention from the tax scandal, the NBA insisted. Even so, the timing was terrific. The decision to elevate Palmer and Kantner ranks among the top officiating stories of the century.

Quickly, the questions and fears arose. Would they be respected, or treated differently from male officials by players? How would the officials handle the antics of Dennis Rodman or Charles Barkley? Before the season, Barkley said, "I don't think women belong there, just like I don't think a woman's place is in the military. Where is woman's place? Behind her man."

Kantner and Palmer answered those questions and more during an October 29 press conference conducted by the NBA. These are some excerpts:

Q: How are you going to handle guys like Charles Barkley, Dennis Rodman and Anthony Mason?

Palmer: We would treat them like any other players. Dee and I are both referees, and confrontation is part of being a referee. If they cross a line that they're not supposed to, they would receive a technical foul, like any player would.

Kantner: Or like any male referee would handle them if they went off. We're given skills to handle confrontation, and we hopefully won't have to utilize them very often.

Q: Talk about your experience handling NBA players, particularly with regard to sexist remarks on the court.

Kantner: I'm not a Pollyanna, but I haven't heard any comment of a sexist nature.

(In her first NBA camp, a player challenged Palmer's foul call. The player, a reserve who rarely played, told Palmer that her call "wasn't an NBA call." Palmer told him he wasn't "an NBA player.")

Q: You probably didn't begin your careers interested in altering history, but you must recognize you have a place in history now. How do you feel about that?

Kantner: I don't think Violet or I could ever say this was our intent, to be trailblazers, per se. If one of the aftereffects is that women are given opportunities that weren't there before, I think we're both in favor of that.

Q: Often when women make advances into men's realms, it comes with a fight or a lawsuit. This really hasn't gone that way. What kind of fighting did you have to do to get here?

Palmer: I think we were selected based on our abilities. I don't think either of us had to fight to get to this point. We were chosen, we were selected based on our ability. Obviously, our ability has spoken for us; otherwise, we wouldn't have this opportunity. No, it wasn't a big fight.

Kantner: (Female sportswriters) are also in the realm that is typically not female, either. If you do your job well, you will be rewarded. Hopefully, that's the same situation we've encountered here.

Q: Do you think you'll be accepted by the players?

Palmer: I think we already have been. I think the only surprise, really, is coming from the fans. Dee and I have been in the program for the last three years, so half of the players in the league either know who we are or have heard something about us.

Kantner: Acceptance is something that Violet and I won't be extremely overtly concerned about.

Q: Some people around the league have gone on record as saying you may not have been the most qualified candidates for the job, that there may have been some men in the CBA who were better qualified. How do you answer those statements?

Palmer: That's their opinion. There is no question, Dee and I know exactly where we stand. The NBA obviously knows where we stand and that's all that matters.

Q: Are you surprised by the attention you have received? Are you embarrassed, or flattered, or wish it would go away?

Palmer: Yeah, I'm a little flattered. No. I'm not embarrassed. I think it's really nice that the NBA is letting us talk to you and hopefully, after we talk, we can just go out and do our jobs. We'll become normal referees in the NBA and work hard just like all the guys on the staff.

Kantner: First of all, normal referees is an oxymoron. I really was surprised that this was front page news. I think Violet would support this, that we just pursued a path that was laid out for us. Sometimes I'm stunned by the response that this is bringing from people.

Q: You were both officials for women's NCAA basketball. Did you try officiating for men's Division I games?

Palmer: I was contacted last year by the Big West Conference to officiate men's basketball. I was told that I needed to go to a men's camp, which I did. I was told that I would receive games and actually work the upcoming season. Then, when it came time for scheduling, to make a long story short, they pretty much copped out. I think it was a matter of not wanting to deal with the pressure.

Kantner: In 1990, I had the opportunity to do an exhibition game at LSU. Coach Dale Brown was very serious about getting me in the loop. I went to camp, and similar to Violet's story, not a whole lot happened from that. So when the NBA came knocking, we responded.

Q: Rookie referees are left alone by the older officials. Are you concerned about that? Do you think the older referees will be supportive, or is there a certain amount of time where you will have to prove yourself?

Kantner: As far as I've encountered, the older referees have been extremely supportive, beneficial and invaluable.

Palmer: I totally agree. They have actually been outstanding in their support, their knowledge and how freely they are giving us the information that we need as rookies.

Q: Violet, can you compare the pace of the NBA games to the WNBA? How did you prepare for the change?

Palmer: There is a big difference, obviously, because we're talking about men and women. Of course, men are larger, faster and their athletic ability is just tremendous. It's just a different game. But it's still basketball. One thing we always have to

193

remember is basketball is basketball, and that's where our training comes in, to get us prepared for this kind of basketball. For the last three years, that's what we've done, and now we're having that opportunity.

Q: Will (your) calls be under particular scrutiny from players and fans?

Kantner: Obviously, we will be different from the other referees. It'll be easier to spot which working officials we are. As far as the scrutiny is concerned, perhaps. But hopefully, as Violet and I do our jobs the way we're supposed to, that scrutiny will dissipate.

Palmer: We are rookies and I don't think that has anything to do with gender. Rookies have to earn their respect and that's what we're going to have to do. We're up to the challenge.

Q: Dennis Rodman said, "They have to be able to run with us on the court, get touched and even patted on the behind every now and then." Can you handle that? If that happened during a game would you consider that sexual harassment?

Kantner: Hardly. If it is in the context of the game, athletes touch on the butt. You know, I never thought at age 37, I would be answering these types of questions. But no, this is not something we are going to misinterpret. If there are actions that are intended to be condescending, I think Violet and I will be, I hope, able to handle them accordingly.

Q: Did men officiate WNBA games?

Kantner: Yes, we had 13 women and 11 men officials (in 1997). Did anyone object? As far as the supervisory position I had, I just wanted to get the best officials on the floor regardless of gender. That's what I think the NBA is doing now.

Q: At what point in your mind and heart did you feel you were good enough to aspire to this level?

Kantner: I think after the first two years of training. The first summer was a shell-shock summer, just trying to get used to the style of play and the difference in rules and getting acclimated to the differences between the games. The second summer, there was a little more of a comfort zone, then I started to realize, "Hey, I can do this." So I would say after that second summer of training, I had confidence this was a job I could accomplish.

Palmer: I agree.

Q: Are there any other women currently officiating who you feel are worthy of officiating in the NBA? What is it about you that has gotten you to this point?

Kantner: As far as other women out there presently, I don't know if either Violet or I are qualified to answer that question. I know Violet and I have been involved in the women's game for years and I believe we're seasoned enough that the NBA felt we were perhaps ready.

The hubbub died down soon after the season starter, and after two seasons, Kantner and Palmer retained their NBA status. Pats on the butt did not become an issue. Rodman, Barkley and Mason made the usual spectacles of themselves, but didn't direct antics at the women officials.

The NBA was widely hailed for breaking the gender barrier, although a woman had previously officiated a professional game. Sandhi Ortiz-DelValle worked a United States Basketball League game in 1991. She also wanted to work in the NBA and filed a discrimination suit against the league, asking for $2 million and a job.

Ortiz-DelValle didn't get the job, but a New York jury concluded she was discriminated against and awarded her a whopping $7.85 million.

"I can't believe (the jury) understood, because so many people didn't," Ortiz-DelValle said.

Kantner mentioned the game she worked at LSU. It actually was a historic occasion. Dale Brown was eager to see women break into the field and in cooperation with the Southeastern Conference, arranged to have an entire women crew. Besides Kantner, Patty Broderick and June Courteau worked the 1990 exhibition game against an Australian club team.

Women officials also made inroads in ice hockey, when 10 females were assigned to call the women's ice hockey at the 1998 Winter Olympics. Vicki Kale, Deb Parece and Evonne Young called games, along with women from Canada, Germany, Switzerland, Norway and Finland.

Young and Parece worked the first game between Sweden and Finland. Parece was the lone American working the gold medal game.

For years, it seemed baseball would precede other sports in hiring women on the major league level. After Gera's attempt, three others tried to break through —Chris Wren, Theresa Cox and Pam Postema. However, only Pam Postema made it beyond Class A.

Chris Wren lasted three years in Class A in the 1970s. When she got her fourth straight Class A assignment before the 1978 season, Wren resigned.

Theresa Cox worked in the Arizona League in 1989 and 1990 before she was released.

Postema broke into pro ball in 1977 and moved up to Class AAA in 1983. She remained there seven years, getting only a taste of the major leagues during some 1988 spring training games. She and seven other umpires were released after the 1989 season. Postema filed a federal sexual discrimination charge against the National and American Leagues in 1990. It was settled out of court seven years later.

Soccer moves forward

Women referees worked the first women's World Cup soccer matches in 1995 in Sweden. Fourteen of the 25 officials were women, and Sweden's Ingrid Jonsson became the first woman to referee a FIFA final, when Norway won the World Cup title. Women officials also called men's games in the 1996 Olympics.

"Good old male chauvinist Baron Pierre de Coubertin (modern Olympics founder) would have turned over in his grave," wrote former referee Michel Vautrot for *FIFA Magazine*. "(He was) the man who was ever a declared opponent of women's participation: 'A female Olympiad would be impractical, uninteresting, unaesthetic and improper.' "

Pierre de Coubertin would have been spinning in his grave had he seen the 1999 women's World Cup in the United States. All officials were women. FIFA officials believed there were enough good women to call the action. They used the event to encourage women to take up officiating.

Women made their debut in Major League Soccer in 1998. Sandra Hunt was the referee in a game between the Chicago Fire and Kansas City Wizards. Nancy Lay worked a game between the Dallas Burn and N.Y./N.J. MetroStars. Both had tough games.

Hunt tossed one player from each team for violent conduct. Lay tossed a Burn defender for a violent tackle. Both women worked MLS teams in the preseason training camps and had worked international matches during the U.S. Women's Cup in 1998.

Not all soccer leagues welcomed women officials with open arms. In 1997, a defender for the Montreal Impact of the A-League, John Limniatis, unleashed a series of expletives and gender-biased comments toward referee Sonia Denoncourt after a game. In a symbolic gesture, the league stripped Limniatis of his defender-of-the-year award.

Based on her experience, it's no surprise Denoncourt was undaunted by the episode. In 1994, she was one of three women appointed to FIFA's list of line officials. In 1996, she became the first woman to officiate an Olympic soccer game. Two years later, she was the only women in the world refereeing Division One men's games.

"I don't know why I have been the first woman so often," Denoncourt said. "It's weird. I don't like to say I've been lucky because I think I deserve everything I've gotten. I was at the right age when changes started. And I was really fit. Fitness is so important to FIFA. They're really, really strict about it, and if we don't pass their tests, we lose our referee's badge. Also, they like the way I run — like an athlete."

Chapter 7

HALL OF FAME

Officials have been included in almost every major sport's Hall of Fame, the notable exception being professional football. In alphabetical order and by sport, here are the enshrinees, the year inducted and why they are considered the best of the best.

BASEBALL

Al Barlick (1989)

Barlick was named the game's best all-around arbiter in 1961 in a poll of players and managers by *The Sporting News*. However, he blasted the story, saying it was a "disgrace ... the very idea of ratings is unfair in that they place labels on hardworking officials who always try to do a good job." There wasn't another poll until 1999.

But in 1970, Barlick gladly accepted the Umpire of the Year award from the Al Somers Umpire School, because it was a poll of umpires.

Barlick worked seven World Series and seven All-Star Games. He first came to the majors in 1940 when he substituted for an ailing Bill Klem. He became a regular the following season.

Barlick left a lasting impression on the Milwaukee Braves, who thought Barlick held a grudge against them. The feud reached a climax after one game, when a naked Barlick charged into the Braves locker room, challenging anyone present to a brawl.

Nestor Chylak (1999)

In addition to his Hall of Fame honor, Chylak won the Purple Heart and Silver Star for heroism in World War II. Chylak was struck by shrapnel from an exploding German shell at the Battle of the Bulge, and nearly lost his eyesight.

Chylak worked in the American League from 1954-78 and called five World Series and six All-Star Games. He was widely regarded as the top umpire of his generation and won the Al Somers Award in 1972.

He made the call to forfeit a game to the Texas Rangers in the infamous "Beer Night" incident in Cleveland in 1974, when drunken fans charged the field in the ninth inning.

Chylak died in 1982 at age 59.

Jocko Conlan (1974)

Conlan is the only umpire in history to make his debut in a major league game. It happened in 1935. Conlan, playing for the White Sox, was fooling around in the clubhouse and broke his thumb. Chicago was in St. Louis for a doubleheader when umpire Red Ormsby suffered heat stroke in the opener. Conlan offered to fill in. "I couldn't play anyway," he told umpire Harry Geisel and the managers.

Managers Jimmie Dykes of the Sox and Rogers Hornsby of the Browns agreed, and Conlan's officiating career commenced that day. He worked the bases wearing a White Sox uniform. Conlan finished the series, then began officiating full-time in the minor leagues the following year.

Conlan arrived in the National League in 1941 with a kick. Literally. He became famous for a shin-kicking encounter with Leo Durocher. Conlan also was noted for his polka-dot bow tie. He was chosen to work in six World Series and six All-Star Games.

In 1967, Conlan wrote his life story, *Jocko*, co-authored by Robert Creamer. It's worth reading. Leo Durocher gets hammered, as you might expect. But so does Jackie Robinson, whom Conlan called "difficult." Conlan may be the first person who, in his final analysis, comes down hard on the player whose number was universally retired by baseball.

"Jackie could never accept a decision," Conlan wrote. "He was more like (Ty) Cobb in temperament and style than any other player. He was very intense. Almost every time he was called out on strikes or on a close play on the bases, there seemed to be words."

Tommy Connolly (1953)

An Englishman, Connolly never played baseball. He had been a cricket player as a kid. When his folks migrated to Nattick, Mass., Connolly was appointed batboy for the local team. In 1894, he called his first game in the New England League, where he was spotted by famed 19th century umpire Tim Hurst. From there, it was a short jump to the American League.

Connolly wasn't a showman. He dressed neatly and wore hard collars. His tie was held in place by a jeweled stickpin. Players respected his no-nonsense approach.

When his 27-year career ended in 1928, Connolly went to work as the American League umpire-in-chief, essentially the umpire's supervisor, from 1931-1954. Connolly spent much of that time scouting talent and was responsible for locating many of the umpires who started in the American League during that era.

Connolly's name surfaced in news reports in 1999. His will, along with those of Boston-area players, turned up on the sports memorabilia market. The case involved the theft of court papers bearing the signatures of Hall of Famers George Wright, Tommy McCarthy, Hugh Duffy and Connolly. A collector bought Connolly's will for $300.

Billy Evans (1973)

Evans never played the game, but was a young star as an umpire, getting the major league call at age 22. He entered the profession after working as a sportswriter in Youngstown, Ohio.

A tough call against the home team in a 1905 Ohio-Pennsylvania

League game precipitated his rise. Watching the game was St. Louis Browns manager Jimmy McAleer, who informed American League President Ban Johnson of this tough-minded prospect. Shortly thereafter, Evans made the longest jump in officiating history, advancing from Class C to the majors.

Evans' career highlights included the plate assignment when Walter Johnson made his debut and when Babe Ruth slugged his 60th homer in 1927. Lowlights included a pop-bottle missile that struck him during a game in St. Louis. Evans was hospitalized, hovering near death for several weeks, but refused to press charges against the 17-year-old perpetrator. Ty Cobb once invited Evans to a brawl under the Washington grandstands in 1921, after he called Cobb out stealing second. Evans, a one-time boxer, accepted the challenge, but was pummeled. After the fight, Evans went into the Tigers clubhouse and shook Cobb's hand.

Because of the influence of Billy Evans, baseball doubled its umpire presence. He was working the bases (with Bill Klem behind the plate) in the 1909 World Series, his first. For the second year, two extra umpires were assigned the Series, kept in the stands as reserves.

Temporary stands were erected to hold the overflow crowd in Pittsburgh. In the opener, the Pirates Dots Miller hit a line drive that bounded the stands in right field. Evans asked the crowd whether it was fair or foul. When they told him fair, Evans awarded Miller a ground-rule double. AL President Ban Johnson demanded an explanation. Evans said he needed the eyewitness assistance, and suggested the two umps in the stands would be of more value on the field. Johnson reassigned the backup umps to the field for the rest of the series, and the four-umpire system became standard in 1910.

Evans moved into the Indians front office in 1927, and later worked for the Red Sox. He became president of football's Cleveland Rams in 1942, but returned to baseball four years later to work for the Tigers.

Cal Hubbard (1973)

Hubbard lives in the Halls. Besides his enshrinement in Cooperstown, Hubbard is a charter member of the Pro Football Hall of Fame for his career as a two-way performer in the 1920s and 1930s with the Giants, Packers and Pittsburgh Pirates. He is also enshrined in the College Football Hall of Fame. Hubbard played for Centenary College, then transferred to Geneva College. In 1926, Hubbard nearly single-handedly led his team's upset of mighty Harvard in the opening game.

When he began his umpire career in the minors, Hubbard continued to play pro football. He moved up to the American League in 1936, and developed into one of the most respected officials in the game. Hubbard took advantage of his 6'4", 250-pound build; he took grief from nobody.

Hubbard's baseball career ended prematurely. While hunting in his native Missouri in 1951, a pellet bounced off a rock and struck him in the eye, impairing his vision. AL President Will Harridge appointed him supervisor of officials in 1954, a position he held until 1969.

Bill Klem (1953)

Much was reported about Klem in the history chapter of this book, and he may have been the greatest ever. But he was wrong in a 1951 *Sporting News* article where he criticized fellow ump Hank O'Day, who called Fred Merkle out for not touching second base in the famous 1908 decision that cost the Giants the pennant. "I never would have made that decision," Klem said.

It's been speculated that O'Day's call kept him out of the Hall of Fame because of the criticism of New York sportswriters. Klem's comments didn't help.

In 1928, Klem threatened to quit when two years passed without a World Series assignment. He was then given three World Series nods over the next four seasons. He worked a record 18 World Series. Klem raised the dignity of the profession by demanding increased salaries and adequate locker facilities. He was animated and imitated, the first to shout out strike calls and waving the arms on foul balls.

Bill McGowan (1992)

Fans don't pay to see the umpire, but they made an exception in the case of Bill McGowan. He was the most colorful umpire in the game when he retired in 1954 after a 30-year career. He died that year at age 58.

Late in his career, McGowan's antics got him in trouble. In 1948, he threw his ball and strike indicator at Senators pitcher Ray Scarborough and allegedly cursed other Washington players. He was suspended for eight days and fined $500 by AL President Will Harridge.

Four years later, McGowan banished a Tigers player who was taunting Browns pitcher Satchel Paige in the dugout. St. Louis writers called the field from the press box, demanding an answer. McGowan turned to them and shook his fist, but never revealed the guilty party (pitcher Billy Hoeft). He was suspended for four days.

These momentary lapses should not detract from his phenomenal career. From the start, McGowan built a streak of 2,541 consecutive games (16 seasons) without missing an inning. He worked eight World Series and four All-Star Games. He also founded one of the original schools for aspiring umps.

BASKETBALL

Jim Enright (1978)

There was a time sportswriters commonly doubled as officials. The rationale for this double-duty was that a reporter was supposed to be an impartial observer and possess some knowledge of the game. Nobody pulled off the double more successfully than Enright.

On a snowy evening in 1930, the 19-year-old Enright, making $15 a week as a sportswriter for the *Benton Harbor News-Palladium* in Illinois, was asked to call a junior high game when the regular official was caught in a snowstorm. Enright made $5 for a 24-minute game. That night, he decided to supplement his journalism income.

Enright had previous experience calling games. He was the umpire and scorekeeper for the House of David barnstorming baseball team. However, he made a career calling basketball. For 34 years, Enright called games in all the major Midwest conferences, while maintaining his job as a sportswriter. He covered the Cubs and White Sox for the *Chicago Evening American* from 1937 until he retired from journalism in 1974. He then spent three years as the public address announcer for the Cubs at Wrigley Field.

Enright earned a spot in the Hall for his outstanding 34-year officiating career. He was in such demand that one year, he was summoned from covering the Cubs spring training in Arizona to call a Kansas-Missouri season-ender that would determine the Big Eight championship.

Enright was big, weighing in at 260 pounds, and loud. "It may be showboating," he once said. "But I want the stands to know exactly what I'm calling and on whom. The gestures are very helpful, particularly when the fans are booing or cheering."

The highlight of his career came in 1954, when Enright called the NCAA championship game.

George Hepbron (1960)

Hepbron, a New York City native, was probably basketball's first referee. He recalled the first time he was employed specifically to work a game — 1893 in Brooklyn. James Naismith had traveled from Springfield, Mass., to talk about the rules, but the players wouldn't tone down their rough play.

"He hated to penalize athletes," Hepbron said. "As a minister, he could see no wrong in the mind of a person. But somebody had to cut down the big men, so the job fell to me."

Hepbron and Luther Gulick wrote the first *AAU Guide* in 1896, basketball's first encompassing publication. Hepbron also authored the game's first basketball methods book, *How to Play Basketball*, in 1904.

The first AAU tournament in Brooklyn exceeded its scheduled time because Hepbron disqualified so many players. In those days, disqualification meant the offending players were out of the tournament. The event was postponed until replacements were found.

Hepbron was the first secretary of the AAU basketball committee, and in 1915, became first secretary of the National Basketball Rules Committee.

George Hoyt (1961)

Hoyt's officiating career began a decade after Naismith invented the game. Around New England, it was Hoyt, not the inventor, who was known as "Mr. Basketball."

Hoyt founded the Massachusetts officials board in 1920. He was fiercely dedicated to his profession, often traveling to remote areas to conduct officiating clinics. His book, *The Theory and Practice of Basketball Officiating*, was one of the first that applied specifically to his profession.

"There's room in the game for the little guy," and, "Basketball is a game of science, not brute strength," were two of Hoyt's pet phrases.

Hoyt started his 34-year career in the 1910s. Comparing the referee to a knight, he once wrote that early officials "... had to have everything except the armor and spear — these too would have come in handy at times."

Pat Kennedy (1959)

Kennedy was the first official enshrined at Springfield. He was probably the best-known whistle-blower of the first half of the century because of his antics and dramatics. Kennedy's showmanship often startled players and coaches the first time he worked with them, but everyone respected his ability.

Kennedy started officiating at age 20, and called up to 150 games a season. He once estimated he officiated more than 4,000 games. He also spent seven years calling games for the Harlem Globetrotters. When he retired from active duty, Kennedy became the NBA's first officials supervisor.

Of all the characters in the game's history, Kennedy may have been the most colorful. He would rush to the scene of the infraction, pointing and screaming even for the most innocuous crimes. "Oh, no you don't, I caught you that time," was one of his favorite lines.

A New York columnist once wrote, "You are told people went to Madison Square Garden, first to see Mr. Kennedy officiate and second to watch the basketballers play. Mr. Kennedy does everything but throw himself through the hoop."

Lloyd Leith (1982)

Leith got his start in officiating because he thought he could do better than what he'd seen as the coach of Balboa Mission High in San Francisco. By 1940, he was working the college ranks. He called games until 1965, when he retired as dean of West Coast referees, while continuing his career as a coach.

The high point in Leith's career came when he called the 1951 NCAA championship game. In all, Leith called 16 NCAA tournaments and 10 national AAU tournaments.

After retiring, Leith served as the NBA supervisor of officials. But when illness curtailed that job, he continued to grade and scout officials.

How have things changed? After working a Cal-Stanford game, Golden Bears coach Nibs Price blew up at Leith and told him he did a lousy job. Leith said, "If Price feels his team would win if I wasn't calling the game, then I should get out. I don't want to be the cause of any team losing a game." The conflict soon was cleared up.

Red Mihalik (1986)

By the time his career ended in 1972 with a knee injury, Zigmund "Red" Mihalik was considered one of the world's best officials. His career started in 1935, when officials failed to show up for a high school game. Coincidentally, his college officiating career started the same way. In 1946, he was a last-minute substitution for a Penn State-Pitt game and earned praise by both coaches afterward. He was immediately recommended for a position in the ECAC.

In 1951, he was named the nation's top referee by a major magazine.

Known as a big game official, Mihalik called six NCAA championship finals, three NITs and the Olympics in 1964 and 1968. He was the first American official to work a game involving the Soviet Union, when he called the USSR-Brazil game in the 1968 Olympics.

John Nucatola (1977)

Called the "greatest official" by Hall of Fame coach Clair Bee, Nucatola worked college games for nearly two decades before moving to the professional game. He was on the NBA's original staff in 1946.

Nucatola served as the supervisor of officials for the Ivy League, the old East Coast Athletic Conference and the NBA. He dedicated his life to improving officiating, conducting more than 1,200 clinics in his career.

Nucatola was one of the earliest advocates of a three-official system and actively worked to get a third official on the floor in the later stages of his career as a supervisor.

"It costs more money, but I'm convinced it works," Nucatola said in 1970. "One criticism is it will result in more fouls, but our study shows games with three officials are averaging fewer fouls."

Eventually, all major college ranks went with the third official.

Ernest Quigley (1961)

Quigley knew a little about the game: He played basketball under Naismith at Kansas. He also played baseball, and after suffering a broken hand in that sport, Quigley turned to officiating. He called more than 1,500 games, including the 1936 Olympic final, and served as director of officials for the NCAA tournament from 1940-42.

In 1913, Quigley branched out, becoming a National League umpire. During his career, he called 5,400 games and six World Series. As a football official, he called more than 400 games, including three Rose Bowls.

As a basketball referee, Quigley was known for shouting in a high-pitched tone, "You can't do that!" and for patting the guilty party on the back instead of blowing his whistle for a foul.

After he called his final game, Quigley became the athletic director at Kansas.

According to *The Sporting News*, "With the possible exception of Bill Klem, no National League umpire of his day commanded as much respect as Quigley."

James Dallas Shirley (1979)

Nobody knew the rules like Shirley, one of basketball's most popular officials. He traveled the world calling games and conducting clinics, and was considered the profession's foremost authority on mechanics and techniques.

In his 33-year officiating career, Shirley called primarily in the

East and South, and was often a post-season choice. He was the only American invited to serve as a referee for the 1960 Olympics.

Shirley was a member of the NBA's original crew, but after only a few years, he chose to call college games instead of the pros. His career highlight was the 1960 Rome Olympics.

Perhaps no official remained busier after retirement than Shirley. He held five part-time jobs after hanging up the whistle.

"I was an extrovert — loud, semi-demonstrative, more so than the average (official) today," Shirley told *Referee* magazine in 1985. "I was not a showboat. I sold the call with confidence, but did not attract all the attention to myself."

Earl Strom (1995)

Strom is the first official elected who is better known for his work in the professional ranks than college. Strom worked 29 seasons in the NBA and three in the ABA. He also called more than 50 games in the finals of the pro ranks. He officiated the entire 1961 finals between the Celtics and St. Louis Hawks.

"In my judgment, Earl was simply the best official to work the NBA," said former NBA coach and Celtics great Bob Cousy. Strom worked more than 2,400 regular season games and 295 playoff games in his career.

Strom was known as a nonconformist and therefore, wasn't popular with some of his colleagues. He argued with fans and once yanked a sportswriter out of his press row seat. Strom and others shook up their ranks when they jumped to the American Basketball Association. He was anti-union and anti-Darell Garretson, the former NBA's chief of referees. In his book, *Parting Shots,* Strom did just that, taking the game and some fellow officials to task.

Dave Tobey (1961)

Tobey was New York basketball's best official in the key growth stage from 1926-1945. As the game's popularity swelled, so did demand for Tobey's talent. He called in the pro ranks from 1918-26. However, after calling a critical Syracuse-Army game in 1926, Tobey became a top college official.

Tobey was on hand for the important games in New York. When he stepped down to return to coaching, Tobey was considered the top official in the game.

Tobey is credited with writing the first book exclusively about basketball officiating, entitled *Basketball Officiating,* published in 1943.

David Walsh (1961)

Walsh was an official/coach, calling high school, college and pro games primarily in the East while coaching Hoboken High School in New Jersey from 1911-1933. He became a leader in officiating and served as supervisor of the East Coast Athletic Conference officials.

While serving as an assistant to Asa Bushnell, Walsh scouted and nurtured the development of so many officials, Hoboken became known as a "cradle of officiating." Fellow Hall of Famer Pat Kennedy and NBA official Matty Begovich hailed from there.

WOMEN'S BASKETBALL

Darlene May (1998)

The inaugural class included May, who was the first woman to officiate an Olympic game in 1984. She also had a 519-119 career record in 20 seasons as a coach at the Division II level.

ICE HOCKEY

Neil Armstrong (1991)

Armstrong once went 16 years without missing an assignment. In all, he officiated 20 seasons, 1,733 games in the regular season, 208 in the Stanley Cup playoffs (48 in the finals), and 10 All-Star Games. He started officiating at age 15 and made it to the NHL in the 1957-58 season.

John Ashley (1981)

In 1971, Ashley became the first official to referee the seventh game in each of the three Stanley Cup playoff rounds that went the distance. His NHL career started in 1959. Over the next 12 years, he handled 605 games as a referee, including 59 in the playoffs. When he retired in 1972, he was considered the game's top official.

Bill Chadwick (1964)

The only American-born official in the Hockey Hall of Fame in Toronto and the only referee in the United States Hockey Hall of Fame, Chadwick is credited with developing the hand signals used by today's officials. For holding, he grabbed his wrist. For tripping, he slapped his shin. Coaches, players and fans first thought he was showboating, but the gestures soon caught on. Chadwick said he developed the system because he didn't know what to do with his hands while skating.

Chadwick spent one year as a linesman, 1940, then moved up to referee. His career started when he was playing with the Stock Exchange team in the Metropolitan League. During a game, he was sitting out with injuries and asked to sub for a ref who never showed. He worked several amateur games in New York, where he was spotted by an NHL observer.

John D'Amico (1993)

D'Amico was the last of the "Original Six" officials. He worked his first NHL game in 1964, when it was a six-team league. When he retired in 1988, there were 26 teams. During a 1982 game in Toronto, D'Amico was hit with a puck that broke his arm. No matter. He continued to officiate the game. He worked more than 1,700 games in the NHL, primarily as a linesman.

D'Amico worked more than 20 Stanley Cup Finals, seven All-Star Games, four Canada Cup tournaments, the Challenge Cup of 1979 and Rendez-Vous '87.

Chaucer Elliott (1961)

Elliott was an all-around athlete a century ago, who settled on a career as a hockey referee in 1903. He was widely regarded as the game's first great official. His 10-year career ended abruptly when he died of cancer in 1913, at the age of 34.

Few early officials were more respected than Elliott, who was in great demand throughout Canada for his service.

George Hayes (1988)

Hayes was the first official to work more than 1,000 NHL contests. In a career that spanned 20 years, he officiated 1,544 games in the regular season, 149 in the playoffs and 11 All-Star Games, primarily as a linesman. One of the game's most colorful officials, Hayes was fired after the 1964 season for "gross insubordination," when he refused to take an eye test. Hayes claimed if he could read labels on beer and liquor bottles, his eyes were fine.

Fellow Hall of Famer Red Storey referred to Hayes as "... the best and most colorful linesman ever to work in the league. He had the highest respect from fans, players and fellow officials."

Bobby Hewitson (1963)

Hewitson was Canada's most versatile official and sportsman. Besides working for 10 years in the NHL, he officiated football and lacrosse. He also played all three sports. After leaving the ice and fields, he worked as a sportswriter in Toronto.

Bobby served as the first curator for the Hockey Hall of Fame and Canada's Sports Hall of Fame.

Mickey Ion (1961)

Many of the game's top officials learned from Ion, probably the best on the ice in the 1930s. He refereed the memorable Howie Mornez Memorial Game in Montreal in 1937. Ion and Chaucer Elliott were the first officials inducted into the Hall of Fame.

Ion began his career on the West Coast and caught the eye of Lester Patrick. He became the top official in the Pacific Coast League, and joined the NHL when the PCL folded.

Matt Pavelich (1987)

The nine officials enshrined before Pavelich were referees. Pavelich, who retired in 1979, spent most of his 1,727 games of the regular season, 245 of the playoffs and 11 All-Star Games as a linesman.

Pavelich started working midget games at 14. He joined the NHL in 1955, after working in the American Hockey League. He broke the NHL record for officials when he worked his 148th Stanley Cup playoff. Pavelich is the brother of former Red Wing Marty Pavelich.

Mike Rodden (1962)

Rodden was elected to the Hall of Fame as an official — he refereed nearly 3,000 games overall, 1,187 in the NHL — but was known for his all-around versatility. He coached two football Grey Cup champions and 27 championship teams and was a successful hockey coach.

J. Cooper Smeaton (1961)

Smeaton chose to officiate rather than play hockey, and there were few better in the first half of the century. He worked as a referee, then briefly as a coach of the Philadelphia Quakers. When the Quakers withdrew from the league, Smeaton returned to officiate in 1931, when he was appointed referee-in-chief.

Smeaton kept that job until 1937. In 1946, he was appointed trustee of the Stanley Cup.

Red Storey (1967)

A knee injury ended Roy Alvin Storey's football career, the pinnacle of which occurred in 1938, when he scored three touchdowns, including one on a 102-yard run, for Toronto over Winnipeg in the Grey Cup.

When his playing days ended, Storey worked as a football, lacrosse and hockey official, serving in the NHL from 1951-1959. He was considered one of the most colorful officials in hockey history.

Frank Udvari (1973)

Only three years after refereeing his first minor-league game, Udvari made it to the NHL in the 1951-52 season. He worked 718 regular season games and 70 in the playoffs before retiring in 1966, when he became the league's supervisor of officials. Udvari previously held the same position in the American Hockey League. In 15 seasons, Udvari missed only two regular season games.

Udvari was at the Nassau Coliseum in New York to watch an Islanders-Atlanta Flames game December 30, 1979, when he made history. During the game, referee Dave Newell received a severe cut and couldn't continue. Minutes later, Udvari, at age 55, was on the ice, wearing a pair of skates loaned by New York star Brian Trottier.

SOCCER

Michel Vautrot (1998)

Vautrot joined such soccer luminaries as Pele and Franz Beckenbauer in the inaugural class of the International Football Hall of Champions. Vautrot, a FIFA referee, served on the referee committee that determined the officials working the 1998 World Cup in France. He retired as a referee in 1990, and worked two World Cups.

Jack Taylor (1999)

Taylor, an English FIFA referee, became the second official inducted into the International Football Hall of Champions. He began refereeing in 1947, and started his international career in 1963. He's best known for his role in the 1974 World Cup final between Holland and Germany. Taylor awarded Holland a penalty kick before the German team had touched the ball when Johan Cryuff was tackled. He scored on the penalty kick, but the Germans won, 2-1.

BOXING

Arthur Donovan (1993)

The first referee enshrined in the Boxing Hall of Fame in Canastota, N.Y., may be better known today as the father of former Baltimore Colts lineman and TV funny man Artie Donovan.

Arthur Donovan refereed 14 heavyweight championship fights from 1933-1946. He called 20 Joe Louis fights, including both with Max Schmeling. In his day, Donovan was boxing's most popular referee and was often asked for autographs. His father was middleweight champion, Mike Donovan.

Ruby Goldstein (1994)

Goldstein was an accomplished boxer from 1925-1937. His referee career started in the Army, and his first heavyweight match came in 1947. He officiated the first Joe Louis-Jersey Joe Walcott fight, and in those days, the official acted as the third judge.

The two ringside judges scored the fight in Louis' favor, while Goldstein scored it for Walcott. Most observers agreed with Goldstein — even Louis defended Goldstein's reputation. He went on to work the first Tony Zale-Rocky Graziano middleweight fight and the Sugar Ray Robinson-Joey Maxim light heavyweight title bout.

Goldstein retired from the ring in the early '60s, one match after officiating the Emile Griffith-Benny "Kid" Paret fight in which Paret died in the ring.

Arthur Mercante (1995)

Mercante worked 114 world championship fights in a career that started in 1954. He got into boxing while serving in the Navy under Gene Tunney as a recruit training specialist. One of his duties was to referee service bouts.

Among his most famous title fights: the second Ingemar Johansson-Floyd Patterson match, Joe Frazier's decision over Muhammad Ali, George Foreman's defeat of Frazier and an Ali-Ken Norton battle.

Mercante's son, Arthur Jr., is one of boxing's top referees. He called the controversial Lennox Lewis-Evander Holyfield decision in 1999 and well as the Sugar Ray Leonard-Terry Norris super welterweight match in 1991.

George Siler (1995)

America's first great boxing referee. Siler refereed boxing when the Marquess of Queensberry rules were first introduced and while the sport was evolving from bare fists to gloves.

Siler officiated the James J. Corbett-Bob Fitzsimmons heavyweight title fight in 1897 in Carson City, Nev. He also called Fitzsimmons-James J. Jeffries and Jeffries-Tom Sharkey, all heavyweight fights in which the title changed hands.

Siler had a reputation for honesty, and wrote about boxing for several newspapers before he died in 1908.

COLLEGE FOOTBALL

The National Football Foundation has recognized an outstanding official, primarily a college official, each year since 1984. To qualify, officials must have called at least 100 college games and contributed to the game after or in addition to their officiating career. They're honored at the College Football Hall of Fame in South Bend, Ind.

1984 John Waldorf
1985 Ellwood A. Geigas
1986 Jack Sprenger
1987 George Gardner
1988 Joseph McKenney
1989 Wilburn C. Clary

1990 Pete Williams

1991 John J. Daly and E.C. "Irish" Kreiger

1992 No award given

1993 John Adams

1994 Ken Faulkner

1995 Bobby Gaston

1996 Earl Galdeira

1997 Ron Abdow

1998 Bradley Faircloth

1999 David Parry

PRO FOOTBALL

There are no referees in the Pro Football Hall of Fame. They are eligible and some have been nominated. The only member associated with the profession is Hugh "Shorty" Ray, who served as an officials' supervisor for 15 years beginning in 1938.

Ray was a four-sport star at the University of Illinois and a high school football coach for 20 years. He was discovered by the Bears' George Halas and became the first person in football to evaluate officials. Ray attended games with a clipboard and stopwatch, always critiquing. He frequently tested his officials and demanded they score at least 95 percent every time.

GOLD WHISTLE

The Gold Whistle Award is presented annually to an official recognized for community involvement, achievement in officiating and reputation for strong integrity and ethics.

1988 Art McNally, former NFL director of officiating

McNally was selected for his long career and professional approach in officiating and public education.

1989 Ed Myer, amateur football official

Myer made a career of training officials, in addition to calling games for more than 50 years.

1990 Pete Pavia, basketball official

Pavia's fundraising efforts helped benefit a Rochester, N.Y., summer vacation facility for disabled children.

1991 Larry Barnett, American League umpire

Barnett was recognized for his long record of voluntary service in the nation's Veterans Administration Medical Centers through the Disabled American Veterans organization.

1992 Jim Tunney, former NFL referee

Tunney has devoted much of his spare time to fundraising and charity work for the Special Olympics, the Los Angeles Boys' and Girls' Clubs and the Family Service Agency.

1993 Steve Palermo, former American League umpire

Palermo and his wife Debbie founded the Steve Palermo Foundation for Spinal Cord Injuries to raise funds for research, equipment and support for uninsured victims of spinal injuries.

1994 Ron Asselstine, former NHL referee

Asselstine instituted the Make-A-Wish Foundation in Guelph, Ontario. In 13 years, the program has raised nearly $500,000, and granted nearly 100 wishes to children suffering a terminal or life-threatening illness or injury.

1995 Ed Hightower, basketball official

Hightower, a school district superintendent, developed a successful after-school program, which has become a model for other schools.

1996 Bernie Saggau, Iowa High School Association executive director

Iowa has established the Bernie Saggau Award that is presented annually to a graduating student of each high school in the state. Saggau is a noted motivational speaker and leader in higher education.

1997 Ted Butcher, amateur sports official and trainer

Butcher, from Holden, Mass., was honored for his years of community service, directing youth programs, training officials, advising college athletic departments and directing clinics for referees, coaches and players.

1998 Durwood Merrill, American League umpire

Merrill developed the Hooks Christian Service, a charity that provides food, toys and clothes to nearly 200 impoverished families every Christmas in his Hooks, Texas, hometown.

1999 Tommy Nunez, NBA referee

Nunez was recognized for his work as the founder and coordinator of the National Hispanic Basketball Classic in Phoenix. The tournament started in 1980 to raise funds for academic and athletic activities for at-risk kids. Nunez also conducts free basketball clinics, and is a motivational speaker.

Chapter 8

ZEBRA TALES

THE AMAZING, AMUSING AND UNUSUAL

Many of us have memories of officials that are, for the most part, negative. We only remember them for the *wrong* they did. Well, there are a few humorous and offbeat stories which make umpires and referees all too human. And sometimes they screw up and get in trouble, too!

The Bain of their existence

In a 1982 Big Ten basketball game, official Jim Bain called a foul in the final three seconds that led to a Purdue victory over Iowa. An Iowa company that produces novelties and souvenirs was upset at Bain's call, so they distributed T-shirts emblazoned with a likeness of Bain's face in a noose. Bain filed a lawsuit to stop production.

The company filed a countersuit of "officials malpractice" and alleged the "negligent call" prevented Iowa from reaching the NCAA Tournament, thus depriving the company an opportunity to sell more Iowa items. A judge dismissed the company's claim.

Wrong way, Red

Red Cashion's 25-year career as an NFL official ended after the 1997 playoffs. He is remembered as one of the greatest to wear the stripes, but even the greatest have their embarrassing moments — the best know how to handle them. Cashion had just concluded the coin toss of the 1986 Super Bowl between the Bears and Patriots. He ran to the goal line for the kickoff, but he ran to the wrong end of the field. He was supposed to stand behind the receiving team. Instead, he found himself having a conversation with Patriots kicker Tony Franklin.

"He says, 'Red, what are you doing down here?'" Cashion recalled. "I said, 'Tony, pretend we're talking about something, like I'm giving you instructions, and everything will be fine.'"

Praying for a zebra

A crowd of 58,000 was never so silent. During a 1997 football game between North Carolina and Virginia in Chapel Hill, N.C., referee Jimmy Knight collapsed on the field and suffered a massive heart attack. The game was stopped for nearly a half-hour as EMT's worked to save Knight's life. (They did.)

The history of officiating is filled with stories of abuse by fans, players and coaches. But this was humanity at its best. After the players knelt in prayer, the game resumed. Coaches informed players to not make officials an issue. Hundreds of students who attended the game signed get well cards, and the hospital received more than 1,000 calls of support. Suddenly, how a game was called didn't seem so important.

Fate in fans' hands

Alex Levinsky scored to give the Chicago Black Hawks a 2-1 lead over the New York Americans in a Stanley Cup semifinal game in New York. But the goal light didn't go on, so the referee skated over to the goal judge to inquire. As it turned out, a group of New York fans has grabbed the goal judge's hands and prevented him from turning on the goal light. The goal stood.

Tainted officials?

You need an abacus to count the tirades of Indiana coach Bobby Knight. One of his most damaging displays wasn't in the form of an outburst, but was a conversation with ESPN analyst and former Notre Dame coach Digger Phelps. In light of recent gambling scandals that rocked college athletics, Knight suggested the players weren't the only guilty ones.

"You and I have always thought this. The most susceptible guy in any gambling scheme is an official, without question," Knight said. "I mean, if we only knew the truth about the games that were controlled by officials having gambling interests, I think it would be amazing."

Hank Nichols, NCAA national coordinator of men's officials, was understandably furious.

"He either needs to come forward with specific names and games, or he needs to retract his comments," Nichols told *The Indianapolis Star.* "This is outrageous."

Of course, Knight retracts nothing. He didn't apologize. He wasn't suspended by Indiana or the Big Ten. Worst of all, ESPN didn't challenge Knight on the spot or in a follow up interview.

Then again …

Maybe Knight knew what he was talking about. In 1957, a Missouri Valley Conference referee, John Fraser, worked nine consecutive games in which large amounts of money were bet on one side. In each game, there was major fluctuation in the point spread. The "smart money" won eight of the nine games. At mid-season, league officials had gathered enough evidence. Fraser was reported to have suffered a mysterious neck injury and was forced to resign.

Land of the rising shove

Mike DiMuro was the first American umpire to work in Japan. After a shoving incident, don't expect many to follow.

DiMuro was behind the plate for a 1997 game between the Chunichi Dragons and Yokohama Bay Stars. He called a third strike on Yasuaki Taiho of the Dragons, who didn't like the call. So he argued, was joined by several teammates in surrounding DiMuro, then shoved DiMuro in the chest.

The Central League served Taiho with a reprimand, but didn't suspended him. DiMuro, who had worked in the American minor leagues the previous five seasons, decided to pack his bags and head home.

A taxing business

Joe Crawford was one of several NBA officials who lost their jobs over tax evasion. He cashed in his first-class airline tickets for cheaper coach tickets, pocketed the difference and didn't report the income. His unpaid income tax amounted to $24,000 over three years. When the IRS found out, Crawford not only lost his officiating job, he had to pay $108,000 in back taxes and fines, and was put under house arrest for six months.

Unlike others who were caught, Crawford issued a statement of apology.

"What was stupid is I didn't have to do it; we didn't need the money. We don't live extravagantly. I did wrong. I don't want anyone feeling sorry for me."

In all, 11 current or retired NBA officials were indicted for tax fraud. Those who were working either resigned their positions or took leave pending the outcome of their investigation. The NBA hired back seven: Crawford, Mike Mathis, Jess Kersey, George Toliver, Don Vaden, Joe Forte and Hank Armstrong.

A Green monster

Former Boston Red Sox standout Mike Greenwell found himself in the middle of an embarrassing episode in 1999, when he twice was ejected from Little League games.

Greenwell, coaching a team of 9- and 10-year-old All-Stars in Fort Myers, Fla., was tossed out by volunteer umpires for allegedly using vulgar language.

Your goal, my goal

January 26, 1921, the Ottawa Senators led the Montreal Canadiens, 3-2, in the third period when Ottawa scored a goal, or so the Senators thought. Goal judge Riley Hern said the puck never entered the net, and referee Cooper Smeaton refused to allow the goal.

A few minutes later, Montreal rushed the net, but Harry Mummery was 30 feet offside. No call. Mummery slammed into goalie Clint Benedict as Odie Cleghorn fired in the game-tying goal. Smeaton allowed the goal.

The Senators refused to take the face-off in protest. Smeaton dropped the puck and Montreal's Newsy Lalonde skated untouched into the Ottawa zone. As he wound up for the shot, Benedict stepped aside and allowed the puck to zip through the unguarded net.

Ottawa let it happen again to make it 5-3, and most of the Senators left the ice. Smeaton declared the game over. The tough part for Ottawa: Lalonde's goal gave him the league scoring title by two points over the Senators' Cy Denneny.

Legal for a day

Coaches Kevin Loughery of the New Jersey Nets and Hubie Brown of the Atlanta Hawks like to sneak in an illegal zone defense now and then. Official Richie Powers surprised them both in a 1978 game when he invited the coaches to play all the zone they wanted. The teams did. Powers was fined $2,500 and suspended for three weeks by the NBA.

Tough guy

During a 1964 heavyweight fight between Ernie Terrell and Bob Foster, the face of Hall of Fame boxing referee Arthur Mercante intercepted a hard blow from Foster intended for Terrell. Mercante didn't go down, continued to officiate and eventually stopped the fight to protect the battered Foster.

Foster was angry the fight had been stopped, but his manager told him Mercante was right because his best shot of the night couldn't knock down the referee.

Saint referee to you

In 1965, Greek soccer official Constantine Fatouros thought he was going to be killed — lynched, to be more precise, after calling a game in which the home team lost.

Fatouros was saved by disguise. He found a priest's outfit, complete with a head-covering cassock, and managed to slip out of town.

Enough fightin' Finley

The AFL had a referee named Bob Finley. As it happened, some of the roughest brawls in football history took place with Finley in charge. The Jets and Raiders engaged in two savage games in the late 1960s. He worked the Chiefs-Raiders game in which Ben Davidson hoisted Len Dawson and speared him into the turf.

Impostors by rule

January 15, 1983, a snowstorm blanketed Hartford, Conn., and referee Ron Fournier and linesman Dan Marouclli couldn't reach the Hartford Civic Center in time for a game between the Whalers and New Jersey Devils. Hockey dipped into its rule book, and applied rule 36(k): "If through misadventure or sickness, the referee and linesman are prevented from appearing, the managers or coaches of the two clubs shall appoint a player from each side who shall act as a referee or linesman; the player from the home club as referee and the player from the visiting as linesman."

That night, linesman Ron Foyt made it, and he served as referee. One player from each side served as linesman. Hartford defender Mickey Volcan and New Jersey winger Garry Howatt, who were nursing minor injuries, put on sweaters and sweat pants and filled the bill, which amounted to calling offsides and icing. There were no incidents.

Two helmets means tails

Famed NFL referee Jerry Markbreit earned his first Super Bowl assignment in 1983, when the Dolphins met the Redskins. On one side, the ceremonial coin had two helmets — that meant tails. The other side had two players holding helmets for heads.

Markbreit flipped the coin, and Miami captain Bob Kuchenberg called tails. The coin landed on the side with the two helmets.

The Dolphins had won the toss. But a confused Markbreit turned to Redskins captain Joe Theismann, and informed him the Redskins had won the toss. Honorary captain Elroy "Crazy Legs" Hirsch stepped in and corrected Markbreit, and head linesman Dale Hamer helped Markbreit sort things out. "I felt like crawling out of the stadium," Markbreit said.

Gifts? Oui, oui

A soccer agent told a French court that he aided the attempted bribery of referees with offers of gifts and women before European Cup matches in the 1980s.

Apparently, the Bordeaux team believed it was robbed by an official's decision in a 1981 European Cup match, and vowed never to let it happen again. From 1983-1988, the club reportedly spent $800,000 on referees. The agent, Ljubomir Barin said, "Bordeaux would offer fur coats, shirts, gifts for the kids. Sometimes girls, too, I don't deny it. All the European referees wanted to come to Bordeaux."

Also used as flotation device

A chest protector probably saved the life of a Little League umpire in Sacramento, Calif., in 1998. Gunfire came from a nearby house, and one of the bullets caught the umpire in the chest. The protector took the brunt of the hit as the bullet grazed the umpire's shoulder. He didn't seek medical treatment.

Best of the minors

Umpire Harry "Steamboat" Johnson worked more than 5,700 minor league games from 1910 until 1946. He tasted the major leagues for only 54 games in 1914, as a fill-in for an ill National League regular. He may have been the best umpire in minor league history. He certainly was the most colorful.

On "Chief Meyer Day" in Buffalo, he tossed Chief Meyer out of the game. He once finished a game with one good eye after a four-inch gash closed the other on a collision at the plate. Johnson used to carry around a medical note certifying his 20-20 vision. Later in life, he covered the date with his thumb.

But Johnson loved his profession and was proud of its integrity.

"I am happy to tell you there is no single instance on record in the history of the game, when an umpire has been charged with and proved guilty of any serious charge of dishonesty," Johnson wrote in his 1935 autobiography, *Standing the Gaff.* "The best umpire in the world might not shine as a scholar in a gathering of college professors, but he could outclass the entire faculty of any university in America in promptly deciding the fine points of a game of baseball."

Dishonesty, yer out!

In 1882, Richard Higham became the only umpire fired for dishonesty. He was a former manager and player from Troy, N.Y., who advised gamblers how to bet on games he was calling.

FAMOUS LAST WORDS
Words of wisdom by/about officials
and their profession.

"Ballplayers don't know anything about umpiring ... There is nobody, just nobody who knows anything about umpiring except the umpires. That goes for commissioners, league presidents, owners, managers, players and bat boys. And the bat boy may know just as much as any of them. I forgot to include fans and sportswriters. Put them on that list, too. They don't know anything about umpiring, either."

- Umpire Jocko Conlan, 1967

"The life of an umpire is by no means a pleasant one. He has but few friends among the fans, and he is often misused by the best of fans. The umpire is something like a Pullman porter, no matter how bad you are mistreated and misused by fans, you must not lose your head. He must be neat, dress like a big leaguer on and off the field; no matter how rank some of his decisions have been, he must do his best and try not to even things up."

- *Kansas City Call*, 1923

"Managers only argue on days which end in the letter 'Y.' "

- Ron Luciano, AL umpire

"Ideally, the umpire should combine the integrity of a supreme court justice, the physical ability of an acrobat, the endurance of Job, and imperturbability of Buddha."

- *Time* magazine, 1961

"Any time I saw those 'bang-bang' plays at first base, I called 'em out. It made the game shorter."

- Umpire Tom Gorman

"I've been mobbed, cussed, booed, kicked in the ass, punched in the face, hit with mudballs and whiskey bottles, and had everything from shoes to fruits and vegetables thrown at me. An umpire should hate humanity."

- Joe Rue, AL umpire

"If the Pope were an umpire, he'd still have trouble with the Catholics."

- Beans Reardon, NL umpire, 1980

"Give or take a few, one-third of all umpires in the National League are incompetent."

- Maury Wills, 1976

"Officiating is the only vocation performed before the public where the only accolade is deadly silence."

- Dolly Stark, umpire

"You fat pig. Have another doughnut."

- New Jersey Devils coach Jim Schoenfeld to referee Don Koharski after a 1988 Stanley Cup semifinal

"I've been the target of 4,000 bottles, 20 of which found their mark."

- Steamboat Johnson, minor league umpire

"A crooked umpire ... is as offensive as a scoundrelly jurist on the bench. When gamblers went to fix a World Series, they did not try to make a deal with the umpires. They knew the umpires would turn them down and turn them in."

- Steamboat Johnson

"He should concentrate on his 3-5 record and let the umpires do their jobs."

- NL umpire Bruce Froemming on ump-griping Expos pitcher Jeff Fassero

"These guys are a little bit higher than the Pope. When the referees come out, they are very powerful. Then they will go back to their business and make about $12 a week and come out again next week."

- Tampa Bay Bucs coach John McKay, 1980

"Many fans look upon an umpire as sort of a necessary evil to the luxury of baseball, like the odor that follows an automobile."

- New York Giants pitcher Christy Mathewson, 1914

"I think what disturbed Richie the most was that he punched the guy and didn't hurt him."

- Former NBA referee Sid Borgia on fellow ref Richie Powers, who was attacked by a fan in Boston during the 1976 finals

"The umpire's first decision was usually his last; they broke him in two with a bat, and his friends toted him home on a shutter."

- Mark Twain, *A Connecticut Yankee in King Arthur's Court*

"It is a team that has nothing more to gain than the abiding respect and recognition of the game itself."

- Michel Vautrot, Hall of Fame referee on the 1998 World Cup officials

"When a good young player misses an unmissable goal chance, nobody thinks of dropping him like a hot brick, kicking him off the entire squad and refusing even to pay his salary. But when the man with the whistle makes a mistake, it too often only serves to reaffirm his incompetence and dishonesty in the eyes of the public."

- Michel Vautrot

One day the Devil challenged the Lord to a baseball game.

The Lord, smiling, proclaimed: "You don't have a chance.

I have Babe Ruth, Ty Cobb, and all the great players up here."

"Well," snickered Satan, "I've got all the umpires."

- Folktale

"Kill him! Kill the umpire!" shouted someone on the stand

And it's likely they'd have killed him had not Casey raised his hand.

- Ernest Lawrence Thayer, *Casey at the Bat*, 1888

"We are a necessary evil, and we're at the bottom of the totem pole."

- Umpire John Kibler, 1980

EPILOGUE

Much to the delight of Jerry Seeman, the NFL got through the first half of the 1999 season with no major instant replay controversies. Replay hadn't become the annoying intrusion that marred the 1991 season, when 90 calls were reversed in 224 games. Through the season's first seven weeks, 77 plays were reviewed and 24 reversed.

The baseball playoffs and World Series got through without a major hitch. So did the opening of the NBA and NHL seasons. All was quiet on the college football front.

But some umpires were working behind the scenes in their quest to dump Richie Phillips. In early November, 52 umpires met in Baltimore and emerged confident there was now enough support to form a new union that would be run by umpires with the legal advice of Baltimore-based attorney and agent Ron Shapiro. He helped organize the meeting and advised the dissenting umpires.

The war of words, so damaging to the profession's image throughout the summer, continued. Union president Jerry Crawford fired off a letter to the umpires before the meeting accusing the umpires of neglecting the plight of the 22 arbiters whose September resignations were accepted by baseball.

"At a time when all umpires should be rallying around the 22 and their families as they take on baseball in the fight of their lives, some from within our own ranks feel that now is the time to launch their own campaign to divide us. Baseball must be licking its chops!" Crawford wrote.

John Hirschbeck, a force behind the dissenting umpires, said if a new union is formed, the first priority would be to see about reinstating the colleagues who lost their jobs. "We care about them, their families, their futures," Hirschbeck said.

It was tough going for many of the 22. A few days after the Baltimore meeting, baseball owners asked an arbitrator to throw out the grievance filed by the union in an attempt to regain the jobs. Crawford had asked umpires who worked the postseason to donate their $20,000 in bonus pay toward the union's legal fees.

Those who lost their jobs found themselves in the unusual position of looking for employment, a condition nobody had anticipated as late as July. But there was Bob Davidson, reading sports for a Denver talk radio show. Gary Darling passed the real estate test on his first try and was looking for a job in Arizona. Tom Hallion found a position as a stock broker trainee in Louisville. Others weren't sure what they were going to do. If they lost their arbitration battle, a severance package worth $100,000-$400,000 would kick in. A nice parting gift, but not the security of a $200,000 annual salary some were making.

And, as the off-season headed towards the gray of winter, umpires were calling for change with the rejection of Richie Phillips as the union head. By a 57-35 vote, the umpires overwhelmingly voted Phillips out of office on November 30. He had been their union leader since 1978.

The officiating profession lost a hero when Sid Borgia died in 1999. He was one of the last links to the earliest days of the

NBA, an original member of the officiating staff. Borgia should be in basketball's Hall of Fame not only because he was one of the game's best officials but he survived at a time when pro basketball was just as rough as football or ice hockey.

In the early NBA years a referee survived by being, as author Leonard Koppett put it, "intelligently selective." In the 1940s and 1950s referees often called games under siege. Coaches and players incited home crowds with gestures and shouts, putting more pressure on the officials. The refs were paid by the owners who insisted on getting not favorable calls, which would be dishonest, but no calls. For years, fouls simply weren't called on rebounds. Players barrelled to the basket and offensive fouls were rarely called. In 1951, the home team won 75 percent of NBA games.

Borgia was the ultimate "no harm, no foul" official and rose to the top of his profession. More than most of his peers in those early years, he wasn't intimidated by owners, coaches, players or fans. To Borgia, the game would be called fair and square, even if that meant a police escort out of the gym.

Today, we take fairness for granted. A fundamental belief of any sporting event is that the contest will be officiated to the highest degree of fairness and integrity. The official may not always be in the best position to make the call. A ruling may be challenged. You might even think a ref or ump is incompetent. An official would rather hear that than have his honesty questioned.

For that reason, and not because of a long home run or field goal, a slap shot or follow slam, sports work. Kill the ump if you must. But you better have another one waiting to take his place.

BIBLIOGRAPHY

Janet Bruce, *The Kansas City Monarchs, Champions of Black Baseball* (Lawrence, Kan., University of Kansas Press, 1985).

Andres Cantor with Daniel Arcucci, *Goooal!* (New York, N.Y., Simon & Schuster, 1996).

Steve Cameron, *George Brett, Last of a Breed* (Dallas, Tex., Taylor Publishing Co., 1993).

Jocko Conlan and Robert Creamer, *Jocko* (Lincoln, Neb., University of Nebraska Press, 1967).

Allison Danzig, *The History of American Football* (Englewood Cliffs, N.J., Prentice-Hall, Inc., 1956).

Dan Diamond and Joseph Romain, *Hockey Hall of Fame* (New York, N.Y., Doubleday, 1988).

Orlando Duarte, *The Encyclopedia of World Cup Soccer* (New York, N.Y., McGraw-Hill, Inc., 1994).

Stan Fischler and Shirley Walton Fischler (*The Hockey Encyclopedia,* New York, N.Y., Macmillan Publishing Co., 1983).

G.H. Fleming, *The Unforgettable Season* (New York, N.Y., Simon & Schuster, 1981).

Larry R. Gerlach, *The Men in Blue, Conversations with Umpires* (Lincoln, Neb., University of Nebraska Press, 1994).

Blair Kerkhoff, *The Greatest Book of College Basketball* (Addax Publishing Group, Lenexa, Kan., 1998).

Jerry Markbreit, *The Armchair Referee* (Garden City, N.Y., Doubleday & Company, 1973).

John McGran, *World's Greatest Sports Brawls* (Atlanta, Ga., Longstreet Press, Inc., 1998).

Durwood Merrill with Jim Dent, *You're Out and You're Ugly, Too* (New York, N.Y., St. Martin's Press, 1998).

James A. Michener, *Sports in America* (New York, N.Y., Fawcett Press, 1977).

William Mokray, *Ronald Enyclopedia of Basketball* (New York, N.Y., The Ronald Press, 1963).

Andrew Postman and Larry Stone, *The Ultimate Book of Sports Lists* (New York, N.Y., Bantam Books, 1990).

Benjamin Rader, *Baseball* (Urbana, Ill., and Chicago, University of Illinois Press, 1992).

Beau Riffenburg, *The Official NFL Encyclopedia* (New York, N.Y., NAL Books, 1977).

James A. Riley, *Biographical Encyclopedia of The Negro Baseball Leagues* (New York, N.Y., Carroll & Graf Publishers, Inc., 1994).

Lawrence S. Ritter, *The Glory of Their Times* (New York, N.Y., The Macmillan Company, 1966).

John Thorn and Pete Palmer with David Reuther, *Total Baseball* (New York, N.Y., Warner Books, 1989).